Simplicity

The Fluid Motion Factor Golf Program

ARMINLEAR

Simplicity

The Fluid Motion Factor Golf Program

Steven Yellin

ARMINLEAR

For further information, contact:
Armin Lear Press
825 Wildlife
Estes Park, CO 80517
ISBN: 978-1-7351698-5-9

*This book is lovingly dedicated
to Laura and Chris Wege
and seekers of Truth everywhere.*

Contents

Endorsements.. 1

Foreword *by David Leadbetter*........................ 7

Introduction 9

1: Fluidization 17

2: The First Set of Fluid Cues 35

3: The Second Set of Fluid Cues....... 51

4: The Gap 81

5: The Third Set of Fluid Cues........... 89

6: The Fourth Set of Fluid Cues 103

7: Changing a Swing 117

8: Swing Prison................................ 123

9: Hitting the Wall 131

Author Biography 145

Endorsements

"After going through Steven's program, I realized that when I played my best, I was doing what Steven taught. I just didn't know what it was or how to access it more often. I won 3 times on the PGA tour and 11 times so far on the PGA Champions Tour. I get asked all the time why have I been able to win more on the PGA Champions Tour. This book contains the reasons. Steven's program is a game changer."

Scott McCarron
2019 Schwab Cup Winner

"I consider Steven an essential part of my team, he has helped me take my game and my understanding of this sport and life to the next level. I've used the program to quiet my mind in the most stressful situations, like performing well in a playoff or making a very crucial putt. If you want to learn to quiet the mind on the golf course, to play calmly and to take control over those monster thoughts that paralyze your game, I would totally

recommend using the Fluid Motion Factor program and take control of your mind and eventually over your game."

Gaby Lopez
LPGA Tour Winner

"Steven Yellin has something very special and seems to answer a lot questions about what the better players are really doing different from the average players."

Jim Muschlitz
PGA Professional

"Steven described perfectly what happened to me when I won the 1996 Texas Open where I beat Tiger by one and Jay Haas by two. I became fascinated with his message and I knew almost immediately the Fluid Motion Factor program was more than a theory, but the reality of what happens when we play well. Right now, right here you have the opportunity to learn how to put yourself into the Zone, quiet your mind, and access your very best golf swings more consistently. Since meeting Steven and practicing the Fluid Motion Factor program with every shot I have played, my performance has been as good as it can get."

David Ogrin
PGA Tour Winner

"I have found Steven's Fluid Motion Factor program to be a game-changer. Literally. Our team has used FMF and I can see the simplicity they have gained in their swings as well as the ability to remove the drama from each outcome. FMF is applicable to so many sports and is taught the same way regardless of the sport thus making it the universal key to unlocking the talent we already have. Working with him has been one of the best decisions I ever made in my 35 years of coaching."

MaryLou Muflur
Coach at University of Washington,
2016 NCAA Women's
National Championship Team

"I think Steven Yellin has done something for me that has never been done before—he has answered questions about the game that I have had for 40 years. I have been on the Golf Magazine "Top 100 Teachers" list since its inception in 1992. I have talked to many teachers and psychologists over the years that have never been able to explain the elusive "aha" moments that you describe so well in your program. I think the Fluid Motion Factor program will change how golf is taught and played."

Rick McCord
Director of Instruction
The McCord Golf Academy at Orange Lake

"I was introduced to Steven's program at Rick McCord's academy and since then my handicap went from 6.5 to 1.8. My son also bought into the program and has gone from a 10 handicap to a 5! The best however was during a trip this summer to Scotland, when my son Brandon aced the Postage Stamp at Royal Troon!"

Jeff Waaland
President, Golden Link and Former Pro

"Steven has helped us discover what it really takes to play great golf. What sets him apart is that he not only knows what to do, he also shows us how to do it. Our belief and understanding of a fluid, quiet mind golf can be attributed to our work with Steven and the Fluid Motion Factor program."

Ria Scott
University of Virginia
Head Women's Golf Coach

"I had attempted the PGA Player's Ability Test (PAT) multiple times and was unable to shoot the qualifying score. A week prior to my next scheduled PAT, I was introduced to Steven's Yellin's process. The PAT requires 36 holes of golf in one day. Within the first three holes, I was struggling mentally. I was able to implement the process during that round which allowed me to continue to shoot well below the target score for the entire 36 holes. I shot a 73 to lead the field the first day and then cruised

in with a 75. Most notably, my putting became more fluid and as the day progressed my confidence improved dramatically. I attribute my success to Steven."

Scott Riley
PGA Professional

"Thank you for helping us implement the Fluid Motion Factor program into our team. I believe Fluid Motion is a vital part of our program and our team uses this program daily. It has allowed us to be freer and simpler while executing golf shots under pressure. Fluid Motion has also reinforced the idea that 'our bank account is full' and we have all we need to reach our potential. Thank you so much for being an integral part of our program. I look forward to continuing to hone this skill as a coach and to continue to watch our players implement this into their games. We look forward to having Fluid Motion and you a part of our future success!"

Shauna Estes-Taylor
University of Arkansas Women's Golf Coach

"I have played professional golf for the past 36 years. In my hay day, I played almost 40 tournaments a year (LPGA, JLPGA) from 1982-1993. I am now coaching the University of Miami golf team and still playing the LPGA Legends tour. My entire golfing and coaching career, I have been looking for how to apply all the advice I had been given: get out of my way, stop tripping over

myself, breathing techniques, pre-shot routine—tons of sport psychology books and lots of top sport psychologist advice. With all the advice, no one had the answer "how" to fix it, they just kept saying, "Get out of your way." Since reading your book and spending three great days with you, you have taught me the secret sauce. I understand now how the brain works and how to get in that "zone" mode! You have taught me how to turn the brain off and play with the ability I know I have deep down. That is what getting out of your way is all about! Understanding how the brain functions and how to find that fluid motion has made a huge difference for me. I now know how to get out of my way. I can't wait to use it more, especially in competition.

That is where I can really feel it working.
Thanks for the insight to this amazing brain we are all gifted with. Complicated it is, but impossible to figure it is not. We all have an inner self that is much smarter and wiser, it's learning how to let that inner self flow outwardly to make us the best we can be, not only on the course but also in life!

Patti Rizzo
University of Miami Women's Coach

Foreword
by David Leadbetter

I have known the founder of the Fluid Motion Factor program, Steven Yellin, for a number of years. In an era of technology and an overabundance of golf instruction on the internet, it's very refreshing to read the aptly named book Simplicity. Having taught a variety of golfers, from tour players to beginners, I know how important it is to focus on the basics and fundamentals to build a repeating and reliable golf swing. However, the big issue with golf, because of the stationary ball factor, is that we have time to try and think our way through the swing, which in the space of just over a second can be a disaster. Working on technique in a mirror, doing slow motion swings, doing drills, especially when working on something new is fine but ultimately, especially out on the course, you have to trust it to happen and not try to force it to happen.

I love the old statement by the famous British coach John Jacobs, "paralysis through analysis," which is a virus that most golfers suffer from. In modern vernacular the "vaccine," if you will, is the Fluid Motion Factor program, a natural subliminal way to play the game that Steven describes expertly in this book.

So, if you have struggled with overthinking the game, feeling like you should be better than you are, lacked consistency, then the approach that Steven takes may open a whole new world for you. Many players of all calibers who have used the Fluid Motion Factor program have found the game more fun, less stressful, and are shooting lower scores as a result.

It is a non-cerebral way of playing golf, which many golfers have experienced for a short period of time —probably more by accident than design. Now, with this book you can experience this feeling on a more permanent basis and learn how to play your best golf.

Simply enjoy *Simplicity*.

Introduction

Unfortunately, I remember it quite well. It was a very humbling experience.

I was 14 years old and had just moved to Florida. Where I moved from is a story unto itself. Having grown up during the height of the Vietnam War, my mother was not going to allow any of her four children to be drafted into that conflict, so we moved to Israel in 1966. It was a bold move.

We didn't last long. Six months to be exact. It was too much of a contrast. The heart was certainly in the move, but the day-to-day reality was just too challenging.

I took up tennis quite earnestly while living there. Actually, the word that comes to mind is fanatically. I loved the sport. And I got good quickly. Unlike team sports, where you were somewhat dependent on others for success, in tennis you stood alone and success and failure was on your shoulders and your shoulders alone. I loved that fact. So when we moved to North Miami Beach, the first place I wanted to visit was the North Miami Beach Tennis Center.

That is where the humbling took place.

I walked into the pro shop the day after we moved there, told the wife of the pro that I had just moved into town, was a fairly good player (actually I told her I was a very good player), and asked her if she could set me up with a game. She sized me up pretty quickly, had a wry smile on her face while I was talking and said, "I know just the right player for you, Steven. His name is Mark Joffey. He is two years younger than you, but he would be a good one for you to play."

I thought to myself "Two years younger! This is going to be a cake-walk!"

He crushed me 6-0.

Okay, Mr. Yellin, meet Mr. Humble Pie and welcome to the world of South Florida junior tennis in the late 1960s.

But it was just the kind of world I wanted to live in. It was the breeding grounds for some players that eventually became the best in the world: Chris Evert, Brian Gottfried, Eddie Dibbs, and Harold Solomon, to name a few. I was not in their league, I was a few notches below them for sure, but we played in the same tournaments and I watched them transition from junior players to Wimbledon champions.

I did have my brief moment in the sun. As a senior in high school, I won the high school state singles championship and our team won the state title. It was a great way to end a high school career.

I was all set to play tennis for the University of Miami on a full ride, when the athletic director resigned, and the school put a temporary hold on signing anyone to a scholarship. Meanwhile, since I was a sophomore in high school, the coach from the University of Pennsylvania, Al Molloy, had been in touch with me. During this whole episode with Miami, he contacted me again and offered a free trip to Philadelphia to check out Penn. I thought to myself, why not, so I got on a plane and visited.

I knew within an hour this was where I was going to school. I went to a Harvard/Penn hockey game, played tennis with members of the team, soaked in the college vibes and when I got on the plane to fly home, I was a Penn Quaker, through and through.

I had a good career at Penn. I played #1 singles until I was a senior. That is when Ricky Meyer showed up. He was taller and stronger than me, had a better serve, better volley and knew how to play the game. He eventually would crack the Top 70 in the world and win an ATP tournament. Okay, I knew my limitations, so when he started playing #1, I didn't feel so bad.

I had my best year as a sophomore. At the end of the season, I was named to the All-Ivy team. I only lost one match that year and that was to the #1 player at Princeton. And it was a heartbreaker, 7-5 in the third. Another memorable match occurred in my senior year when we traveled to Port Washington Tennis Club and played a team they had put together. We all figured if we were traveling to a club to play a local team and not traveling to play a college team, then it must be a pretty darn good team.

And they were a good team. A very good team in fact.

By that time, I was firmly entrenched in my #2 position, so I would be playing Port Washington's #2 player. Port Washington had my favorite courts: indoor clay. I was not a big, strong player; I was a small, quick, and smart player. Clay neutralized the big hitters and their big serves, so I always felt I had a chance against them when I played them on clay. On a fast court, there was always the chance they could overpower me. So, when Port Washington's #2 player walked out on the court, I was licking my chops. He was about my size. Perfect.

He hit three shots in the warm-up and my jaw dropped. It only took three shots to see that this kid was something special. Completely below the radar, with the smoothest, most minimal motion I had ever witnessed in a tennis stroke, his balls were coming back to me with the precision of a guided laser. Whoa, I thought to myself. This kid is something else. But fortunately for me, he was still just a kid. Fifteen years old. When we split sets, he went south and I easily won the match. I don't think he won a game in the last set.

But one thing I do vividly remember was the Dunlop Fort racquet he was playing with spent almost as much time out of his hand as in it. It was all over the court. Of course, if you are playing someone losing it every other point, you're loving it. Keep throwing it, son. You can never throw it enough!

Fast forward two years and I am sitting in my

living room watching Wimbledon on TV and that kid I played at Port Washington is playing Jimmy Connors in the semi-finals. His name? John McEnroe. I just about fell out of my chair. Okay, I thought to myself, you are 1-0 against Johnny Mac. Something to tell your grandchildren. I'll just leave the age part out. Makes for a better story.

But something else happened in my senior year; it was something that changed my life and led to the writing of this book. In a very ordinary team challenge match, against a player that I must have played 10 or 15 times and never lost, I slipped into a state that I had never experienced before. It was a state where the magic happens. It was the Zone. Oh boy, was it the Zone!

Now, I was in the middle of the food chain in national junior and collegiate tennis. I would go to the nationals every year, that wasn't a problem, win a couple of matches, but then someone would have Steven Yellin for breakfast and that would be it. But for that one hour on the court, against a player I was very familiar playing, I experienced what the top players in the country felt. And what was that?

Freedom. Absolute freedom.

I could do whatever I wanted to do with the ball, whenever I wanted to do it, and it was ridiculously easy to do so. In tennis, there are very strict boundaries. In golf, you can be on the left side of the fairway, the middle or the right, but in tennis, those service and base lines are always staring you right in the face. But for that one hour, those lines became invisible. For sure I saw them, but I was not a prisoner of them.

I finished the match, sat down, and could not move for ten minutes. I was overwhelmed by the experience. I knew that something special had just occurred, something that would have a huge impact in my life. I didn't know where it would lead or how it would lead me, but I knew my life was going to be different.

It felt like a gift—Nature had opened up its vast and infinite intelligence and said, "Steven, for one hour We are going to give you a very clear experience of what it feels like to have complete freedom when you play, then We are going to close that portal and you are going to have to figure it out."

I was all in.

Eventually I had to get out of my chair and go to class, but I could not let go of this experience. Why did I have it? I had played thousands of hours of tennis, in so many tournaments, against so many different players on so many different surfaces—why did I have this life-changing experience today? What precipitated it? I was determined in trying to understand it and for two or three days, I could not let it go. I had to figure it out. I just had to.

I woke up on the third day and bingo, I had figured it out.

It was black and white with no grey whatsoever. I had experienced something very specific and because of that, my game went to another level. I thought in my 21-year-old mind—an "I could do things very quickly" mentality—that it would take maybe two or three years to develop a systematic method to at least give players a chance to have this kind of Zone experience. Of course, there is no guarantee in this, but at least players would start to be more consistent, which is what they hope for any time they walk on to the court.

I was a little off in the time calculations.

It didn't take a couple of years; it took a lifetime. Why? Simply because that arena in which Zone experiences are generated is a very subtle one and it took a lifetime to fully understand the subtleties of how fluid motion is generated from there.

Now, at this point, you are probably expecting me to describe in great detail why I had that life-changing Zone experience. That would be a logical thought. Well, that is exactly what this book is all about, so fasten your seatbelt as I am not only going to answer that question in a thorough and exhaustive manner, but more importantly, also give you a very specific program so you can move in the direction of having the same kind of experience for yourself. Only instead of teaching it in respect to tennis, I am going to teach you the program in golf. The processes in the mind responsible for producing fluid motion operate identically regardless of what sport you are playing. My program has been taught in twelve sports, as Zone experiences in any sport have the same origin.

Let's dive deep into those processes now.

1

Fluidization

About twenty years ago, I had the good fortune of meeting Dr. Fred Travis. Travis is a neuroscientist who wrote his dissertation on electroencephalogram (EEG) coherence and meditation. Simply put, EEG coherence reflects functional connectivity in the brain, that is, areas of the brain working together as a whole.

Travis is the head of the Center for Brain, Consciousness and Cognition and, since that dissertation, has become one of the world's experts on the effects of meditation on EEG coherence. He has co-authored more than seventy papers on the relationship between Transcendental Meditation and EEG coherence and for five years in the 1990s, he worked closely with the Norwegian Olympic Athletic Committee to study why some athletes consistently medal in international and Olympic games and other athletes, equally talented, do not.

Along with Dr. Harald Harung from Oslo University, he published their findings in a book, *Excel-*

lence Through Mind-Brain Development. Their book documents that excellence in any field is determined by one factor and one factor alone—the level of mind-brain development. Mind-brain development includes higher brain integration, psychological development, and growth of higher states of consciousness. Everyone intuitively knows it is the mind that separates the great from the not so great, but Travis and Harung were the first to clinically prove it.

Over the years, I had the opportunity to spend many hours with Travis. He explained in great detail how fluid motion is produced in all sports and why it shuts down. Because of these conversations, I refined my program to mirror how the brain physiology operates. I owe a deep sense of gratitude to him as I credit these talks for refining my program and making it more powerful over the years.

Fluid Motion—A Generic View

As I mentioned, every athlete, in every sport, produces fluid motion identically. The mind is not concerned whether you are throwing a ball, hitting a serve, or crushing a drive. The dynamics for producing motion are identical across the board. Just as the heart, liver or kidneys work identically for every person, generating fluid motion works identically for every athlete, regardless of the motion. So, let's go into that now.

To produce a motion, any motion, whether it be walking across the street or hitting a golf ball, you have to generate a signal in the brain. In other words, you must generate an intention to do something. There are two parts of the brain that I will initially talk about that are important in producing fluid motion. Don't be concerned: This is not a neurophysiology class. But it is important to understand the dynamics of producing motion if you are going to have a comprehensive understanding of the dynamics of generating fluid motion in your golf swing.

The first part of the brain we'll discuss is the pre-frontal cortex (PFC), or front part of your cortex. It is the CEO of the brain; it oversees all processes occurring in your brain physiology. Essentially, it is the discriminating intellect. When it feels like you are thinking about something, it is the PFC that is doing the thinking.

The second part of the brain is the motor system. When you produce a fluid motion in any sport, the signal during the motion bypasses the PFC and goes directly to the motor system. It is the motor system that communicates with the body to produce a motion. The problem occurs—and it is a mighty big problem if you are a professional golfer—when during the motion, the PFC delays the signals moving to the motor system. In other words, you start thinking too much. Then in the middle of the motion, the body is looking for direction from the mind (guess what, the body does not have any intelligence to initiate a swing!) and there are too many processes occurring. That is when the bulkier, core muscles dominate the motion. The result: You're producing something other than fluid motion.

This good process, when the signal bypasses the

PFC and goes directly to the motor system, I call the Fluid Motion Factor. As we all know, there are many ways to teach someone how to swing a golf club and there are obviously many ways you can swing a golf club. But there is only one way you can produce fluid motion in a swing. The Fluid Motion Factor has to occur in order to produce fluid motion. Since it is the PFC that disrupts producing fluid motion, the goal is to keep the PFC offline. That's it, folks. If you know how to do that consistently you can stop reading this book right now.

Just to show you that fluid motion is produced identically in all sports, if you sat down with a hundred athletes from different sports and asked them how they felt when playing their best, you could probably divide their responses into three categories. See if you can relate to these categories.

1. ***Time slows down.*** During a motion, you feel you have all the time in the world. For instance, you are at the top of your swing, and it feels like you have all the time in the world before you start down.

The experience of time is controlled by neurons in the PFC and neurons in the motor system. When the PFC delays a signal moving to the motor system, the neurons in the PFC will overshadow the neurons in the motor system and you will experience time moving quickly. No one shoots a 65, walks off the course and says time was rushed out there. What do they say? What do you say? Time slowed down.

2. ***It felt like you were not thinking too much.*** The mind felt very quiet and you didn't remember much

about what you did during the motion or even during the round. Everything felt automatic and timeless.

The PFC is the intellect and when it goes online you will remember every detail. No one shoots a 65, walks off the course and said they were thinking a lot during the round. They probably said they were not thinking much at all. These three stories highlight this point.

This is a quote from an interview with Tiger Woods after he first stormed on to the golf scene and rose to the top:

> **"There are many putts or many shots where I don't remember hitting. I remember seeing the ball flight. I remember preparing for the shot, pulling the club out of the bag, and once I'm behind the ball, I'm walking into the shot and I don't remember [anything] until I see the ball leave."**
>
> *("Tiger Woods – Getting in The Zone," www.youtube.com/watch?v=y4Wov4vdCEg)*

Meanwhile you have Jim Nantz or Nick Faldo in the booth, saying, "Look at Tiger's concentration, focus, and determination," but what was Tiger's inner experience? He didn't remember much of what happened. His PFC was offline.

When Bubba Watson won the Master's in 2013, reporters asked him after the round what his game plan was on the back nine. His reply:

> **"I don't remember anything about the last 9 holes."**
> *(www.golfchannel.com/news/bubba-watson-captures-masters-playoff)*

When Maria Sharapova upset Serena Williams in the 2002 Wimbledon finals, the biggest upset in the history of Wimbledon, they asked her after the match, how she did it. Her reply:

> **"I have no idea."**
> *(USA Today, June 2002)*

Get the point?

3. ***The motion felt effortless and the body felt liquid and free.*** "I didn't even feel the club or the putter move" kind of statements comes to mind.

The motor system is composed of three parts, but the real genius of these parts is the cerebellum. The cerebellum does two things:

1. It monitors where the motion is, and where it must be, to be successfully completed. And it has the ability to self-correct the motion if something misfires.

In other words, if you are at the top of your swing and you know the club is not in a good position, if you have accessed the correct use of the cerebellum, it will liquefy the body enough to redirect the club on the way down and square it at impact. The ball may not go as far or be hit as solid, but you are still in the hole, as it will be going straight. If you have not accessed the correct use of the cerebellum, you have to make a perfect move on the ball, as the body will not have any self-correcting mechanisms occurring. Now how many times do even the best pros in the world put a perfect move on the ball? Not many.

2. The cerebellum smooths out a motion. David Leadbetter, one of the greatest teachers in the history of the game, says that a golf swing is a transfer of energy from the lower body, to the upper body, to the arms, hands and then to the club. At each part during a motion, there are transitions occurring. When the transitions are not smooth, it is simply because the cerebellum is not doing its job.

So how important is the cerebellum in a golf swing? Essentially it will determine how far you go in the game.

The buck stops here.

Muscle Memory

Next, let's focus on muscle memory, or if you wish to call it, motion memory. Everyone knows there is something called muscle memory. But the muscles do not have any memory. Muscle memory is located in the part of the brain known as the basal ganglia.

Developing muscle memory is like saving money in a saving bank. Imagine you want to save $10,000. You go to the bank, open up a savings account and start putting your money in. Maybe $200 one month, $250 the next, $150 the next, until finally over a period of time, you have your $10,000.

Now, regardless of when you go to the bank, your money will be there. If you go on Tuesday, your money is there. If you go two years from now, your money is there. If you go **five** years from now, your money is there. It hasn't gone anywhere.

When Dr. Travis told me a neurophysiological fact ten years ago about muscle memory, there was a nuclear explosion in my brain. I immediately realized the enormous implications it had for athletes in every sport.

He said that once someone has grooved their motion, meaning it could be repeated consistently, muscle memory does not break down. What breaks down is the ability to access what you already own.

I immediately realized the implications. Muscle memory is like money in a savings account. Once you have your $10,000, you will always have your $10,000. Once a motion is grooved, meaning when you go to the range and drop a bucket of balls and are consistently hitting the ball well, if that motion breaks down on the course, what really broke down was your ability to access what you own.

This means that you don't have to reinvent the wheel on every shot. You don't have to open a new savings account and start from scratch to save up another $10,000 on every shot. All you have to do is not violate the rules of the bank and you will have access to all your funds, or at least a majority of your funds that will enable you to play well that day. And there are limited rules of the bank! You will learn the rules of the bank in this book.

Here is an example that makes this point clearer. Imagine a very good player is going to play in a very big tournament. Let's say the natural shape on his drive is a draw. He goes to the range before his tee-off time, drops a bucket of balls, works through his bag, gets to his driver and proceeds to hit ten or twelve very acceptable drives. Sure, one or two are special, but he would take any one of them on the course and be satisfied.

Twenty-three minutes later he tees it up on the first tee. He looks out at the fairway and it is not a right to left hole, it is a left to right hole. Ugh. He is playing with three other players and he cannot believe how, with minimal effort, they hit it so pure and far. Ugh. He played this tournament last year and he doubled the first hole. Ugh. He really wants to get off to a good start because then he feels confident in his game. Ugh.

When it's his turn to go, in the middle of his swing, he goes to the teller in the muscle memory bank to withdraw one of those ten or twelve very acceptable drives he hit 23 minutes earlier, and the teller says, "Oh, Mr. Yellin, we are so delighted that you are playing in this tournament, but you have violated the rules of the bank and you do not have access to your $10,000, you only have access to $2,700."

The result is that he does not hit one of those ten or twelve perfectly acceptable drives he hit 23 minutes ago. He pops up some pathetic thing that is 35 yards in back of the shortest drive in the group.

Meanwhile, if he were to turn around 180 degrees and hit a ball into the parking lot, where there is no fairway, no course and no tournament, how many times do you think he would not put a good move on that ball? See the point! If there were something wrong with the swing, there would be something wrong in the swing regardless of where he was aiming. **But there was nothing wrong in the swing because muscle memory does not break down.**

What happened? He violated the rules of the bank. Fortunately, there is a limited number of rules and they apply to every person, performing any motion in any sport. That is why in so many ways this is not my program; it is everyone's program. In this book you will learn all the rules of the bank.

Mind/Body Connection

Our next topic is the mind/body connection. Understanding this relationship is crucial for understanding how to play consistent golf.

The mind has different levels. A good analogy would be to compare it to an ocean. Just as there are surface levels of the ocean, where the waves are choppy and moving rather quickly, there are also deeper, quieter levels of the ocean where there is stillness, silence, and no movement at all. The mind is structured similarly. There are surface levels of the mind, which are characterized by thinking intently, being focused and analyzing situations. The mind also has deeper levels, where it becomes very quiet and silent. We all experience the mind moving from more intense thinking to less thinking every day, perhaps hundreds of time during the day. At night we experience less and less thinking as we try to fall asleep, until the mind settles down to a very quiet state that results in sleep.

The body also has different levels. One can say there are surface levels of the body that are represented by the core, bulkier muscle. These are important muscles for a motion, but if they dominate the motion, you will not produce fluid motion. Then you can file down and say that the ability to fire the fast-twitch muscles and the ability to correct the motion represent the deeper levels of the body's intelligence.

Here is the secret sauce.

When you generate an intention from the surface level of the mind, you only have access to the surface level knowledge of the body. But the mind/body connection is set up such, that when you generate an intention from a softer, quieter level of the mind, you have no choice but to access the deeper levels of the body's knowledge. When someone is having an outstanding ball-striking day, they are generating intentions during the swing from a softer, quieter level of the mind. But when the opposite occurs and they are having a poor ball-striking day, they are generating intentions from the surface level of the mind. This explains why a talented player can play well one day and not the next.

Tiger's year in 2013 is an excellent example of these two scenarios. He won five times that year. He played Bay Hill in Orlando, went through the field like a hot knife through butter, won it and everyone started saying Tiger is back, Tiger is back. Well, Bay Hill was his

67th win on tour. Do you really think it makes a difference if Tiger wins 67, 68 or 69 tournaments in his career? Is that going to make any difference in the history books on how the world views Tiger's career? No, not at all. His place in the annals of golfing greats is secure whether he wins 67, 68 or even breaks Sam Snead's record of 81.

Three weeks later he tees it up at Augusta. This is a different story. This is not 67 going on 68 wins; this is 14 chasing 18 majors—Nicklaus's record.

Tiger could not find the fairway that week. His miss was right and left. He hit the ball beautifully at Bay Hill. Did his swing break down in three weeks? No, it's neurophysiologically impossible for his swing to break down in three weeks, unless he had an injury, which he didn't.

What broke down was where he was generating his intentions to swing. That is why he drove the ball so poorly in the Masters. He wanted to win at Augusta more than he wanted to win at Bay Hill, because he will ultimately be judged by how many major events he won, not how many PGA tournaments he won. Because of that, he was over-focused and over-determined.

As it turns out, it is not what you are thinking that determines from where intentions are generated. If that were the case, swing thoughts would always work. But they don't. And this is why they don't.

Let's say someone's swing thought is full turn. On the fourteenth tee they have that swing thought and just stripe the ball. Best drive of the day. They get to the fifteenth tee and of course they are going to have the same swing thought because it worked so well on 14.

But with the same swing thought—full turn—they hit some pathetic drive that barely goes anywhere. Why did it work on 14 and not 15?

Because it doesn't matter what the contents of your thoughts are. This is counter-intuitive to hear for the first time, but from a neurophysiological perspective, it is absolutely true. If that weren't the case, the swing thought would have worked identically on both holes.

But it didn't and here is why: **It doesn't matter what you are thinking, it matters how you are thinking it.**

This is the subtle, below-the-radar understanding of the mind/body connection and why golfers constantly change swing thoughts. And sometimes even a few times during the round! Here is the sequence.

You have a new swing thought. It is fresh, quiet, and soft and is generated from a deep place in the mind. As a result, it works spectacularly well. So well in fact, that it becomes the star of the show, and starts to be generated from the surface level of the mind. Then it no longer becomes effective. So, what do you do?

You have to start over and think of a new swing thought you haven't used for a while. It is a fresh thought and it is generated from a quiet place in the mind and for a while it works well, until it is generated from a surface level and then it no longer works. What happens then? Once again you go to the well and see what you can come up with.

Really? This is how you want to live your life out

there? Like playing bingo? Every week something new? Hoping and wishing you stumble across something that works?

But this is exactly how professional golfers, in fact just about every golfer lives. Because a thorough and comprehensive understanding of the dynamics that control the swing is just about non-existent to golfers, every week it is a different swing thought, a different story, a different fix. Essentially it is admitting to yourself that you don't really understand the most important element of a golf swing—the dynamics that actually control it.

Could there be anything more wrong with that picture in your life as a golfer?

That is not a good space to be in. In fact, it's a precarious, gambling kind of place to be in. By the end of this book, you will be in a much better place.

There is one goal of the Fluid Motion Factor program. It is the same goal for every player regardless of playing ability:

Access what you already own!

I have asked hundreds of players, from major tour winners to junior golfers, a simple question: If you could access what you already own on a consistent basis, would you be a happy camper at the end of the day? Virtually everyone said, "Yes." It is not to say that you cannot put more money in your bank account. Of course you can and of course you should. But you cannot access what you don't own. Most golfers, even your 16 or 18 handicap golfers, have had shots or rounds where they are very satisfied with the results. They are only thinking, "Let me do that more often." This program will teach you how to do that.

I am going to play the devil's advocate here and ask, What if there are some serious mechanical issues in my swing? Why would I want to access that?" Good question. I have two responses:

1. I have seen many swings self-correct when someone goes through this program. Because the brain physiology is operating from a deeper, more powerful level, it will sync the swing better and self-correct it. Given the chance, the body always wants to default to more powerful and correct positions in a swing, but unless you have accessed the Fluid Motion Factor, it can't. This self-correcting does not happen all the time, but it does happen enough to be a recognizable pattern. But let's say you go through the program and you are doing it correctly and there are still some issues in your swing that need to be addressed. Then…

2. Go see a PGA or LPGA professional ASAP. They can help you in correcting swing issues. That is what they are trained to do.

Priorities of the Program

There are three priorities in the program.

1. The Fluid Motion Factor has to be accessed. This is not an option for golfers, or for any athlete. The signal during a motion has to bypass the PFC and go directly to the motor system. Consistent players have figured out a way to do this, but even their system, if they have a system, sometimes doesn't work. After going through the program, you will have a systematic way to do this. It is not to say it is going to work perfectly every time, but it will greatly increase your chances of becoming consistent.

2. The DNA Goal needs to be buried. The DNA Goal is the embedded goal in a sport, meaning you never have to think about it. For instance, when a basketball player is about to shoot, they never have to be reminded it would be a good idea if the ball went in the basket. Or if a tennis player is serving, they never have to be reminded to get the ball in the service box.

Now let's say you have a 12-foot putt for birdie. Regardless of what is going on in the round—or even your life!—does anyone have to remind you it would be a good idea if you made the putt? No. But the problem occurs when you make the DNA Goal the surface goal: **I have to hit the fairway, I have to hit the green and certainly, I have to make the putt.** Let's call this Plan A. Plan A is: The more important the situation, the more focus, concentration and determination you think is needed.

When you do this, the tendency is to systematically shut down the Fluid Motion Factor. Why? Because the quickest way to shut down the FMF is to have more focus, concentration, and determination than necessary. Then you are giving a green light for the PFC to go online and check to see how you are doing with things.

Remember, the PFC is the CEO of the brain. Just like a real CEO, it wants to investigate and see what is happening everywhere. If you give it the slightest invitation to go online, it will instantly take advantage of that invitation. Plan A sends a handwritten, personally signed invitation for the PFC to go online, analyze everything and mess things up. When you played your best golf, would you say it was characterized by more intense focus, concentration and determination? Probably not. So why would you default to those attributes, especially in pressure situations? You shouldn't.

In this book, you will learn Plan B. Plan B is a much more intelligent plan than Plan A. Plan B is not my plan; it is Nature's plan. It is systematically aligning yourself with how the brain physiology produces fluid motion. Because of that, it greatly increases your chances of playing consistent golf. Of course you need a certain amount of focus, concentration and determination to play consistent golf, but much less than you think. Much less.

For example, when you are playing a practice round and you miss a shot from the middle of the fairway with a perfect lie and you drop another ball in disgust and stick it three feet, did you have more or less focus, concentration and determination on the second shot than the first?

Exactly.

3. **The third priority is there are three paradigm shifts in the program.** These paradigm shifts form the foundation of the program. I never tell someone

what these shifts are, as this is not a program where I am trying to convince someone of something. I am not trying to convince anybody of anything. You have to convince yourself. I just set up the conditions for you to have the experience so you can convince yourself. And these paradigm shifts are game changers. For instance, a typical paradigm would be that if you are traveling to an important tournament and you are thinking to yourself, "If I swing well, I am going to play well." This would be a logical thought process and a standard paradigm. But remember, the money is always in the bank. A more powerful paradigm would be something like, "If I don't violate the rules of the bank and access what I already own, I will play well."

Huge difference.

2

The First Set of Fluid Cues

The Fluid Motion Factor program consists of four sets of Fluid Cues. These Fluid Cues set up by design what normally is experienced by chance. In other words, they set up accessing the Fluid Motion Factor. Each set of Fluid Cues gets more powerful, meaning the second set is more powerful than the first and the third more powerful than the second. But it is important to go through all the sets of Fluid Cues systematically and diligently, as each set of Fluid Cues has a specific goal to achieve in the overall goal of the program.

I don't have to tell you that golf is a brutal sport. Tennis, in my opinion, is a much more "intelligent" sport because you get so many chances. You can be down 0-6, 0-5, 0-40 and come back and win. That happened one year in the first round of the French Open. In the ladies' division, a player was down with that exact score, meaning there was only one small nail left in the coffin and her opponent is done and two hours later she ends up in the coffin.

In golf, it is much different. One or two poor swings and it's over and then it's almost impossible to come back. Think of Jordan Speith on the 12th hole in the 2016 Masters. He puts one in the water, chunks his next, and loses his chance to make history and wear another green jacket.

When it is your time to go, things get very serious. And quickly. Often, you walk into the ball like you are walking into combat. Then you do your little dance over the ball, trying your best to get into a golf state of mind, focusing in on the task at hand, but in that split second, right before you pull the trigger, you know you can't have too much focus, so you try to relax a bit. Sometimes you catch that space and sometimes you don't. If you catch that space correctly, you will have a better chance of hitting a solid shot. (More about that crucial space later.)

Ideally, as soon as you pull the club out of the bag, you should be accessing the Fluid Motion Factor, so when you are over the ball, you are already where you have to be and there is no hunting and searching.

I've asked hundreds of golfers to give me one word to describe how they felt when they played their best golf. Top three answers? Easy, simple and effortless.

When you played your best golf, I imagine it also felt very simple. The whole goal every time you play is to replicate that feeling of simplicity and that is the reason why the FMF program is simple. It must be simple because you never get simplicity from complexity; you only get simplicity from something that is simple. With that thought in mind, here is the first Fluid Cue from the first set of Fluid Cues.

Fluid Cue #1

As soon as you start your pre-shot routine, I want you to start thinking of the number nine. You can think it one time, five times, ten times…you can think it fast or slow, stop or go…it doesn't matter how many times you think it. **The important thing is how you think it.**

As I discussed earlier, there are surface levels of the mind and there are softer, quieter levels of the mind. I want you to think the number so softly that it does not have a concrete form. It is more like a feeling, a faint trace of the idea of number nine. In fact, I want you to think it so softly, it feels like you are not even too sure whether you were thinking it! It could be there; it could not be there. Not too sure.

Once you are over the ball, I want you to still think of the number nine. Then right before you pull the trigger, I want you to stop thinking the number for the briefest of seconds. Then during the swing, I want you to think one long nine. Don't pay attention to where the number stops during the swing. It could stop towards the beginning, at the top, on the way down. It could stop anywhere. You are not paying attention to where it stops, and it could stop in different places on different swings. **Don't look for a pattern.** Be innocent. In fact, it's best not to even pay attention to where it shows up.

There are two tracks you can experience here. The first is if you are not getting good results. You are not hitting the ball better or you may be even hitting the ball worse. If that is the case, I want you to think the number softer until you are hitting it well. Think it *really, really, really* soft. Hardly there.

The second, more common track is you start hitting the ball very well. In that case, this is what to look for.

You will hit maybe one, two or seven or eight, or any continuous sequence of good shots and then you will hit one shot that is totally unacceptable. When that happens, and it will eventually happen, if you are doing the Fluid Cue correctly, it is because you have fallen into one of four pitfalls. Everyone eventually falls into these pitfalls, because everyone, regardless of their playing ability, produces fluid motion identically.

The learning curve is identical regardless of whether you have won a major championship or are just trying to break 90 for the first time.

Here are the pitfalls followed by explanations of each:

1. *You try to own the program.*
2. *You don't allow it to be a pattern-less pattern.*
3. *You make the nines (or any of the FCs) the star of the show.*
4. *You associate specific moods with hitting a good shot.*

You can never own the program.

This is a tough one because this is not how we learn. When we learn and then practice something, we expect to get better. For instance, let's say you are learning French. You learn ten words a day, so by the end of the week you have learned fifty words and by the end of the month, you have learned two hundred words. You are way ahead of where you were on that first day when you did not know even one word.

So now you are practicing the Fluid Cues. You are hitting the ball very, very well. In fact, it could be that you are hitting the best you have ever hit in your life. You are thinking, "This is fantastic! I own this program." But unfortunately, you can never, ever own this program.

The environment from which Zone experiences are generated has specific nuances, specific laws of motion that must be respected. You just can't waltz in, order a drink and expect to be served. You better respect those nuances, or you will be humbled in a second.

That is why Zone experiences are so elusive. If you feel you own the program, meaning you feel you can do the program perfectly every time and expect excellent results, then you will very quickly start generating intentions from the surface level of the mind and not have access to the deeper levels of the body's knowledge.

As soon as you fall into the first pitfall and say, "Yes, I own the Fluid Motion Factor program now and I can do it every time perfectly," you will start generating the nines from the surface level and not from a softer level. As a result, you will not have access to the deeper levels of the brain physiology responsible for producing smooth, consistent swings. This is a bitter pill to swallow, but you must.

It is a pattern-less pattern.

We look for patterns in whatever we do. It is as if each day we are drinking order from the universe, because establishing patterns gives us stability and a sense of control in a fast-paced, always changing world.

But again, the environment from which Zone experiences emerge has its own nuances, its own laws of motion and if you violate these subtle laws of nature, don't expect to get the results you want. One of these nuances is that it is a pattern-less pattern. This means as soon as you feel you have figured out the pattern in the program, you will start generating the nines from a surface level of the mind and not a deeper level.

This phenomenon occurs all the time in golf. I call it the 65-75 syndrome. Players shoot a lights-out round, think they have figured out the pattern that led to that outstanding round and the next day they shoot four or five strokes higher. In the Fluid Motion Factor program, you have to start from scratch on every shot, like you are doing it for the first time. This somewhat goes against how the mind works, but nevertheless it must be done.

Don't make the nines the star of the show.

This is what usually occurs: You do the nines and hit a lot of good shots. After a short amount of time, you feel that all you have to do is the nines and you will continue to hit good shots. Then you start doing the nines from a surface level, and not a deeper, softer level and you stop hitting good shots.

The nines are not like some magical number that will open the doors to golf nirvana. **It is not the number; it is where the number is generated from in the mind that is the secret sauce.** As soon as you make the nine, or any of the Fluid Cues, the star of the show and they start to be generated from the surface level of the mind, you are in precarious waters. Then the subtle dynamics responsible for solid shots and Zone experiences are compromised.

No mood making.

When you start doing the nines, the good shots feel simple and effortless. Because the mind is always looking for a pattern and because you associate feelings of simplicity and effortlessness with hitting a good shot, you start looking for those feelings of simplicity and effortlessness in every shot. In other words, you try to create a mood during the swing. As soon as you do that, you lose your naturalness, and this quickly translates into a lazy, lackadaisical, sloppy swing.

Never try to create a mood. The key word is natural. You must be who you are on every shot and every shot has the potential to feel different. Just like you should not be married to the exact same routine on every shot (more on that later), you cannot be married to having the exact same feelings on every shot. If you try to recreate a mood, you will lose the natural dynamism in your swing. You have to be who you are and who you are may be different on different shots. The singer that comes to mind is Cyndi Lauper, who sings a song called *True*

Colors. Apropos.

If you fall into a pitfall, (and you will and more than once!), do three things to reset the clock on the next shot.

1. *Acknowledge what pitfall you fell into. You don't have to write a research paper on it; just a cursory acknowledgment will suffice.*
2. *Do the FC (in this case the nines), softer. The main reason you didn't hit a good shot was because the FC was generated from the surface level of the mind.*
3. *Bury the DNA Goal deeper. Honestly, does anyone have to remind you that it would be a good idea to hit a solid shot or get it close to the target? Reminding yourself of the obvious will just move you in the direction of generating intentions from the surface level of the mind. Do you remind yourself to drive on the right side of the road?*

Intention is more important than execution.

I am going to give you further instructions on how to do the FC. This will illustrate how subtle the region where Zone experiences are generated truly is.

The intention of doing the FC is more important than whether you actually did it. Please read that sentence again.

With this instruction, you are starting to understand just how subtle the region is that generates 64s and 65s on Tour. As soon as you give the mind something abstract to do, immediately the mind starts to move in the direction of abstraction. When this occurs, you don't have to quantify it or give a report card.

In fact, if you start to quantify it and map it out on paper, the whole environment where Zone experiences are generated can shut down in a nanosecond. The analogy that comes to mind is when you push a boulder off the top of the mountain, gravity will move the boulder downward automatically. You don't have to hope and wish the boulder will find the bottom of the mountain or understand all the nuances of gravity that are at work there.

That is why twelve- and thirteen-year-old kids find that magical Zone experience space more often than when they are nineteen and twenty. There is a certain amount of innocence at those younger ages that is lost when they get older and start over-analyzing what it takes to swing well.

From a practical standpoint, this means if the nines showed up in the pre-shot routine, fine. But if they didn't show up, that's just as fine. If the nine shows up during the swing, fine. But if they don't show up, that's just as fine. You can't lose! **The key point is that as long as you have the intention to do the nines, it makes no difference whether they show up or they don't.** It's a win/win situation. The mind will gravitate towards abstraction as long as you had the intention of doing the nines before the shot.

The intention is more important than the execution. If this approach doesn't soften the sound of the number, you are thinking the number from the surface level of the mind. As soon as you have gone through a few cycles of hitting some good shots in a row and then missing one, and understanding why you missed it based on what pitfall you fell into, then you are ready to move on to the next FC. But do not try the next FC until you have gone through many of these cycles. The temptation may be to try what is next and see if that works better, but I suggest you stay patient.

Fluid Cue #2

Now, instead of thinking nines in the pre-shot routine, we are going to switch things up a bit. I want you to count backwards, 9-8-7 in the pre-shot routine. Just 9-8-7. Not 9-8-7-6 or 9-8-7-6-5, just 9-8-7. Do not go beyond 7, and keep starting over from 9. You are thinking the 9-8-7, in the same way you thought the nines—from a very soft and quiet place in the mind.

Once you are over the ball, continue thinking 9-8-7, and then right before you pull the trigger, you stop for that brief second. Then when you swing, think another 9-8-7, but there are two caveats. The first is you are not trying to get to a specific number, like 8 or 7. On different shots, you may get to different numbers, or in between numbers. Don't fall into a pattern or look for a pattern. Each shot has its own uniqueness.

The second caveat is the 9-8-7 during the swing

needs to be a little softer, just a little softer, than the 9-8-7 in the pre-shot routine. There should be a slight contrast, not a big one. Now remember, as with all the FCs, intention is more important than execution. This means that if the 9-8-7 shows up in the pre-shot routine, fine. But if it doesn't show up, that is just as fine. The same principle applies during the swing. If the 9-8-7 shows up or it doesn't show up during the swing, both scenarios are acceptable.

Practice this FC for a while until you have gone through cycles of hitting a series of good shots and then missing one and identifying the pitfall you fell into. Always remember that intention is more important than execution. Once you have done both FCs, the nines and the 9-8-7, most people will like one over the other. This is normal. In this opening set of FCs there will be ones you like and others you don't. Remember each set of FCs gets more powerful, so you are just warming up here. Think of them as hors d'oeuvres, before the entrée comes out.

Fluid Cue #3

Let's go back to you thinking the nines in the pre-shot routine. Think the nines in the pre-shot routine until you are over the ball and about to swing. Right before you are about to swing, stop thinking the nines, just like in the first FC, and go ahead and swing. You will not think of doing any FC until you are at the top of the swing and then you will think a very soft 8. Then, around contact think a very soft 7.

Remember, intention is more important than

execution. If the nines show or don't show up, or if the 8 or 7 shows up or doesn't show up, it doesn't matter, as long as you had the intention of doing them. Then you are good to go regardless of what unfolds.

Fluid Cue #4

When setting up a shot on the course, you stand behind the ball and visualize what shot you are going to hit. You then walk into the shot, set up and quite often, you look up at the target to make sure you are aligned correctly and are focused on the target (a lot more on that later). When this occurs, looking back out at the target, essentially the mind goes out to the target. And then the mind comes back to the ball. You may do this a few times. Finally, after you have checked the real estate out enough times, you are ready to pull the trigger.

But what sometimes happens is that right before you pull the trigger, the mind goes out to the target again, because you are over-anticipating an action that has not yet occurred. When this happens, the experience of time gets distorted. Ultimately, it is the experience of time that controls the muscles. This is the definition of being in the moment. When there is too much of an over-anticipatory response going on in the mind right before you are about to swing, you are asking for trouble.

Here is the FC: Right before you are about to initiate the swing, after you have checked out the real estate there enough times, I want you to draw an imaginary vertical line through the ball. Before you swing, your attention has to be to the right of that line. Your focus will always be on the ball, because you don't hit a ball with your head looking upwards, but your focus can be on the ball and your attention can be on the target.

If your attention moves a little ahead of the line, that's okay. Don't try to put your attention in prison by forcing it to be absolutely to the right of the ball. If it creeps forward a little, that's fine. And when having your attention to the right of the line, don't try to burn a hole in the ground with an intense gaze, like you are looking for kryptonite. Your gaze should be soft and easy, the same as when you are talking to someone.

After you feel your attention is to the right of the imaginary line you drew, then go ahead and swing. There is no specific FC you do during the swing.

If you do this FC correctly, you should start experiencing time normally, rather than over-anticipating something that has not occurred. You will experience the motion in what I call "real time" rather than "distorted time". This means you will experience the motion at each step as it physically unfolds, rather than over-anticipating something that has not occurred, that is, at the top you are already anticipating how it will feel at impact.

Goals of the First Set of Fluid Cues

Each set of FCs has a specific goal to accomplish in your understanding of how fluid motion is produced and specifically, how it is produced in your swing. The goal of the first set of FCs is twofold:

1. *The startling realization that you don't need to have as many swing thoughts as you thought.* In fact,

it could be that you didn't need any swing thoughts. Most people that have gone through the program start having less and less swing thoughts when they go through the first set of FCs.

I am neutral when it comes to swing thoughts. If you want to have them, fine. If you don't want to have them, fine. Your choice. But what naturally happens to most is that they start to fall away of their own volition. Why? Because you don't have to reinvent the wheel on every shot. You don't have to remind yourself of what you already know what to do. In the second set of FCs, I will talk more about swing thoughts and why sometimes they work, and other times do not.

2. *After hitting well with the feeling that you weren't doing much at all, the game-changing, paradigm-shifting realization dawns that muscle memory does not break down and you don't have to start over on every shot.* *Once the money is in the bank, it's always in the bank.*

This is a huge game-changer. Unless you realize, by having the experience, that muscle memory does not break down, you are probably living in a complicated, complex world of trying to reinvent the swing on every shot. You are most likely living in checklist city. This is one of the main reasons why most golfers do not reach their potential.

This is not to say that you cannot put more money in bank. You always can put more money in the bank, but you cannot access what you do not already own. There is a way to put more money in the bank that is more effective than how is usually done and I will talk more about that later in the book.

If you have not hit enough good shots to realize the validity of the above two goals of the first set of FCs, you are not ready for the second set. If this is the case, that is, you have not hit enough solid shots to arrive at these conclusions, then you are not doing the FCs correctly.

The solution?

Do them more softly than you did them before. The reason you did not have success was because you were generating them from the surface level of the mind, and because of that, you were only accessing the surface level of knowledge of the body. So, soften everything up. How do you do that? You just do it. There is no magic formula, just the intention to think the FCs from a softer place in the mind.

First Set of Fluid Cues—Review

1. ***Nines into the shot***, *pause, one long nine during the swing.*

2. ***Count backwards 9-8-7*** *into the shot, pause and then another 9-8-7 during the shot. The 9-8-7 during the shot has to be softer than the one in the pre-shot routine and it doesn't matter what number you get to.*

3. ***Nines into the shot, pull the trigger and then eight around the top of the swing and seven around impact.***

4. ***Right before you pull the trigger, draw an***

imaginary vertical line through the ball and your attention has to be to the right of the line before you pull the trigger. Attention has to be light, not over-focused.

3

The Second Set of Fluid Cues

Now it's time to get serious. I consider the first set of FCs to be the warm-up act, the hors d'oeuvres before the main course. Most golfers like the first set of FCs because it gives them a wonderful taste of freedom and simplicity in hitting balls, and it begins to move them out of swing prison. The drama starts to fade. But the second set of FCs represents bringing the main course to the table. Here we go.

Setting One

Let's go PS here. Pre-Steven. No Fluid Cues, no Fluid Motion Factor program, no cerebellum. Let's put you back into that space of how you hit balls and played before you picked up this book.

I want you to imagine you are about to hit an important shot in an important tournament. I want you to set up the shot on the range and go through your normal routine. But right before you swing, I want you to drop the club, stand up and just chill there for a second. Just chill.

Now, if this was an important shot in an important tournament and hypothetically, obviously very hypothetically, right before you were about to pull the trigger, you dropped the club and stood up, do you think you would feel a contrast between how you felt when you were about to pull the trigger with the club in your hand versus how you felt when you dropped the club and stood up without the club in your hand? By contrast, I mean how you felt mentally. Do you think you would feel much lighter and at ease?

I believe you would. You would probably feel much lighter and at ease, because after all, you don't even have a club in your hand, so obviously there would be no angst about hitting a shot. The key question to ask: Was there a significant amount of ease and lightness experienced when you dropped the club and stood up? In other words, did you feel almost a sigh of relief when you stood up? Remember, you are trying to simulate what you would hypothetically experience if you did this in an important shot in an important tournament.

Most players I have worked with have said yes, there would be a significant contrast in how they felt if they were about to hit an important shot in a big tournament and they just dropped the club and stood up with no club in their hand.

We are going to do what I call Setting One. Setting One means that right before you pulled the trigger, if you dropped the club and stood up, you would feel more or less the same as you felt right before you were about to pull the trigger. Obviously, you will always feel lighter when you stand up without the club in your hand, but if there is a significant contrast, the Fluid Motion Factor has shut down.

Great ball-strikers Set One naturally and they are not even aware of doing it. Here's why. The first two or three feet of takeaway of the shot are crucial. At that moment, if the shot is not experienced in terms of wholeness, you are rolling the dice as to whether you will be able to access your muscle memory. The opposite of wholeness is thoughts pulsating loudly in your head, such as, "don't hit it right", "don't hit it left", "don't hit it long", "don't hit it short", "get the club in this position". You get the picture.

Wholeness is not the absence of parts. It is the togetherness of all the parts. A good analogy would be making a smoothie. When you make a smoothie, you put in different ingredients: banana, strawberries, raspberries, apples, and so on. Then you hit the blend button. If, after you hit the blend button, you can see the outline of the banana from the rest of the ingredients, you don't have a smoothie.

The same is true when you are over the ball and about to pull the trigger. Let's say you have multiple goals for that shot: two swing thoughts, how you want to shape the shot, how far you want it to go and the trajectory. So, you have five ingredients in your smoothie. If you have not hit the blend button before you pull the trigger and two out of those five elements are pulsating like nobody's business, then essentially it's gambling during the swing. You may or may not accomplish what you want. Why?

If you don't make a smoothie, the cerebellum, which is responsible for syncing the swing, will be challenged to work properly. The cerebellum needs to experience a threshold level of wholeness for it to do its job. If something is pulsating and breaking wholeness, meaning something has become more important than anything else and is trying to be the star of the show, it's questionable as to what will happen.

There is a reason why golfers systematically break wholeness—and it's a paradox. They feel that if they focus more, which tends to break wholeness, they have a better chance of executing. So, they systematically and consciously sabotage themselves on every shot. Of course, they feel the opposite.

There is only one criterion for execution: Did the signal get intercepted by the PFC or did it not? If wholeness is broken, then by definition, an element of the swing allowed the PFC to go online. The PFC, being the CEO of the brain, is always looking for any means possible to get involved. By having a part of the swing or the shot start pulsating or by being overfocused, the PFC gets a green light to go online and mess everything up.

Another definition of Setting One is wholeness. Golfers cannot repeat that word enough times. The brain physiology loves wholeness. It was designed to operate most efficiently when it experiences wholeness. It is weakened when a part of the swing or the shot breaks wholeness, meaning something starts to dominate over something else. An example of this is that you have a driver in your hand and there is OB on the left and your miss is left. You start putting your attention on not missing it left and in so doing, wholeness is broken, and you probably pull it dead left.

This understanding, which is not my understanding, but how the brain physiology produces fluid motion, is a radical departure from how most golfers understand the game. Most golfers feel they must put their attention on one or more elements of the swing to execute. Now, I am not saying that you should not have swing thoughts (Jack Nicklaus had four of them and he did quite well!) or that you should not be thinking about the shape of the shot. What I am saying, and I am saying it in as strongly as possible, is that you better hit that blend button before you pull the trigger and you better make a beautiful smoothie. If not, you may be sitting at a beautiful black-jack table in Vegas.

In my opinion, this is the number one reason why golfers do not improve. They are systematically seeing how much wholeness can be broken before they pull the trigger. In other words, how much can they not Set One. They need to go in the opposite direction. They need to set up the conditions that allow the brain physiology to produce fluid motion, instead of seeing how successful they can be in setting up the conditions to shut it down.

Not to get too technical here, but there are two feedback loops occurring in the brain to produce fluid motion. They are between the basal ganglia, which stores muscle memory, the cerebellum, which syncs the swing and gives the body the ability to self-correct, and the motor cortex, which communicates with the body to produce a motion. If one of those loops is broken, you will never be sure what you are going to get. The only way the loops can be broken is if a part overshadows the whole. In other words, if wholeness is broken.

Setting One is asking yourself an extremely specific question. It is not asking if you are relaxed or feel this is a good time to pull the trigger. It is asking, "If someone took the club out of my hand, would I feel more or less the same?" The key is *more or less*.

There will always be a range you fall into when you do this. Sometimes you will be in the higher range, sometimes in the lower range, but as long as you are in the range, you will be okay. Don't try to feel, for instance, that you have to tune into the exact station on a radio dial. You don't have to tune it to 98.6. As long as you are somewhere in the 98 range, high or low, you'll be fine.

Setting One is the first FC in the second set of Fluid Cues. Do nines into the shot, Set One and swing. No FC during the swing; just nines into the shot, Set One and pull the trigger.

After you hit about ten or twelve shots with this routine, ask yourself this crucial question: **Did you see the correlation between Setting One and the quality of the shot?** Obviously, there are two answers, so let's go down each path.

> 1. *If you have not seen the correlation, that is, when One was set well, you had an excellent*

chance of hitting a good shot, then I want you to turn around 180 degrees and set up without a ball and then Set One. This will give you a baseline of what One should feel like. Now turn back around again, set up with a ball, Set One, hit it, and then grade each shot on a scale of 1-10 on how well One was set.

A 10 would be if someone took the club out of your hand right before you pulled the trigger and you felt more or less the same. A 1 would be if someone took the club out of your hand right before you pulled the trigger and you felt a significant contrast. Obviously, you give yourself the number after you hit the ball.

You do not give yourself a number on how well you hit the shot. For our purposes now, that is irrelevant. Just give yourself a number from 1 to 10 on how well One was set.

If you are self-disciplined in doing this, you will eventually see the correlation between Setting One and the quality of the shot. You should see that it is a one to one correlation, meaning if One was set well, you had an excellent chance of hitting a solid shot. It is crucial to see this correlation and you should not do any more FCs until you have seen this. If you are not seeing this correlation, then every five or six balls, turn around, Set One without a ball and see if there was a contrast between Setting One with a ball versus without a ball. Repeat this until the correlation between Setting One and hitting a solid shot is unmistakable.

2. *If you have seen the correlation between Setting One and the quality of the shot, then you are good to go.*

When you have seen this correlation, **and only when you have seen this correlation,** then you have just changed how golf is played.

When you play, obviously the most important element is the swing. But if you had as much control over the swing as you would like, you would make very few poor swings. We know that doesn't happen.

But you have complete control over something as **important** as the swing and that is how much wholeness you have before you started the motion. If you have a threshold level of wholeness then, you have just doubled or tripled your chances of experiencing wholeness during the swing. If you have not experienced a threshold level of wholeness before you pull the trigger, then honestly, you are gambling out there. The processes not only responsible for syncing the swing, but also for having good tempo and solid contact, have been compromised. Carole King's song *It's Too Late* comes to mind. It's one of my favorites. If wholeness and Setting One is not experienced before you pull the trigger, and then you pull the trigger, then indeed it is too late.

The goal when playing is to set up the conditions in the brain physiology that allow you to play your best. That's it. Remember the swing does not control the swing. **The swing does not control the swing.** Processes in the mind control the swing.

Diverting slightly, the book written by Drs. Fred Travis and Harald Harung, *Excellence through Mind-Brain Development: The Secrets of World-Class Performers (Routledge, 2019)* highlights this point and is a landmark book in sports. The Norwegian Olympic Athletic Committee wanted to answer the following question: Why did one group of athletes consistently medal while another group, equally talented and equally dedicated, did not? After five years of research they came to the unremarkable, but as of yet unproven conclusion, that the group that was consistently medaling in Olympic, European, and national events were experiencing more wholeness in their brain physiology. In other words, the ones that medaled had more efficient brain functioning. The book on their finding should be a must read for every coach and athlete trying to understand the mind/body connection in sports (and in life!).

Now, let's go through all the Setting One FCs. There are four of them. And remember, as with all the FCs, intention is more important than execution. As long as you had the intention of Setting One, that is good enough.

1. *Nines into the ball, Set One, pull the trigger and swing. No FC during the swing.*
2. *Nines into the ball, Set One, and then Set One again at the top of the swing. This means you ask yourself the question in the vicinity of the top of the swing, that if someone took the club out of your hand, would you feel more or less*

the same. And remember, as with all the FCs, intention is more important than execution. As long as you had the intention of Setting One at the top of swing, that is good enough.

If you didn't remember to ask yourself this question at the top of the swing or if you didn't Set One, it doesn't matter, as long as you had that intention before you started your pre-shot routine.

We are working in a very subtle arena here and as long as the mind is moving in the direction of abstraction, you don't have to quantify the results.

3. *Nines into the shot, Set One and then keep One Set for that crucial two or three feet in the take-away. After Setting One for that portion of the swing, don't worry about Setting One for the rest of the swing.*

4. *Nines into the shot, Set One and then keep One set for the whole swing.*

Practice all four FCs until you decide which one you like. Since all of them have the same goal, to produce wholeness before you pull the trigger and to produce wholeness during the swing, it does not matter which becomes your favorite. As long as you have firmly established the correlation between Setting One and the quality of the shot, you are good to go.

Universe One and Universe Two

Put an alignment stick five feet behind a ball you are going to hit. Stand in back of the alignment stick as if you were setting up the shot.

When you are in this position on the course and you are determining what shot you want to hit, you take into consideration all the elements of the shot: lie, wind, shot selection, where you are in the round, and so on. When you do this, you immediately create an algorithm. This algorithm contains all elements of the shot in one formula.

An algorithm is created on every shot. Let's call the space behind the alignment stick Universe One. Once you have created the algorithm, you move forward to hit the ball. Let's call the space when you cross the alignment stick Universe Two. What usually happens to most golfers is they create the algorithm in Universe One and then they remind themselves of what they created in Universe Two. And usually many, many times!

Not good.

There is one goal in Universe One, create the algorithm. Take your time. No one has a gun to your head. Take into consideration all the elements of the shot. Once you have done this and you have stepped over to Universe Two, you have one goal **and it is to create wholeness before you initiate the swing!** Are you going to forget the algorithm in the three or four seconds it takes to make the long journey from Universe One to Universe Two? Are you going to forget which way the wind is blowing or how you want to shape the shot or what kind of lie you have?

Doubtful.

Then why are you reminding yourself of what you already know and is almost impossible to forget? The reason why is that in your understanding of execution, attention equates to execution; meaning that if you put more attention on some aspect of the algorithm, flighting the ball a particular way or getting the club in a certain position, then you have a better chance of accomplishing the goal.

Not so fast. Remember, the brain physiology loves wholeness and is weakened when a part overshadows the whole. Any part. So if your attention is flighting the ball a certain way and a majority of your focus is on that, to the extent that it breaks wholeness before you pull the trigger, then you are living in that random-luck city you don't want to live in—Las Vegas.

There are two facts that every golfer should know and these two facts, unfortunately, are not widely known. The first is that muscle memory does not break down. The second is that brain physiology loves wholeness. Not being fully cognizant of these facts is the reason why golfers remind themselves over and over again of what they created in Universe One, when they step over to Universe Two. They think they have to reinvent the wheel and they don't. They think they have to start from scratch on every shot and they don't. Once the money is in the bank, it is always in the bank. But they don't know that, so what do they resort to in Universe Two?

The checklist. And it is usually a long one. That is where they are putting their eggs and it is not the right basket. The brain physiology loves wholeness and muscle memory does not break down. If that is the case, then what should be the **only goal** you have in Universe Two? **Create wholeness.** That's it. But what do most golfers do in Universe Two? **They systematically see how successfully they can break wholeness!** That is their goal in Universe Two. It's almost their mission. Why should anyone be surprised that many golfers do not improve over time?

There is one goal in Universe One. Create the algorithm. There is one goal in Universe Two. Create wholeness. In this set of Fluid Cues, you have four ways you can create wholeness in Universe Two. They are the four Setting One FCs. Go through all the Setting One FCs and pick the one that feels most comfortable. After you have picked the one that is most comfortable, then here is the FC: After you have set the algorithm, nines into the shot, Set One and pull the trigger. Welcome to the land of wholeness. It's Stevie's world, baby!

Target Fluid Cues

Just because wholeness is established before you pull the trigger, there is no guarantee wholeness will be experienced during the swing. By Setting One, you are simply increasing the chances. Where in the swing do you think wholeness has the best chance of being broken? Probably at the top, because that is when you are initiating the move to hit the ball, so things can get dramatic up there. And what element of the shot do you think usually breaks wholeness at the top? I would say target, because the goal of the swing is hit it to the target. With that in mind, here are two very powerful target FCs to help you with this.

The first is after you hit a ball, give yourself a number from one to five on how much the target broke wholeness at the top of the swing. This may sound abstract to do, but after you hit one or two balls, you will know exactly how much the target broke wholeness. You give yourself a five if the target shattered wholeness and a one if the target never pulsated out of wholeness.

The second FC is hit a ball to a target and then hit a ball to no target and see if there was any contrast between the two swings. Ideally, there shouldn't be. The goal is to feel when you have a target, to have the same swing as when you don't have a target. I have a lot more to say about the target, especially when practicing, but will save that for a later chapter.

The Infamous Dinner Party Story

Here is the most important story in the program: the infamous dinner party story.

Let's say you are having a dinner party and only 25 guests can come to your party. These guests are coming from a combination of two groups of 25. One group of 25 are your best friends and the other group of 25 are people you wouldn't want to spend ten minutes with, so of course you don't want them to come to your dinner party. The only thing you have control of in your dinner party is how to set the table; you know where the plate goes, the fork, the knife, and so on.

After you set the table, you have to stay on the couch and see who knocks on the door from these two groups. But, if after you set the table, you go to the door and see who is showing up for your dinner party, (after all there are 25 people you absolutely do not want to show up!), then 75 percent of the time, the wrong combination shows up.

But, if after you set the table, you stay on the couch, and don't get up, then 75 percent of the time the right combination shows up. How does this relate to hitting a golf shot?

You are never too sure how the shot is going to turn out. If you were always sure, you would never hit a bad shot and we know that doesn't happen. When you play well, there is a certain level of innocence, which indicates you were probably on the couch. Innocence is not a word typically associated with championship golf, but nevertheless it is there. Remember Tiger's quote noted earlier in the book. The essence of it is that he didn't remember anything until he saw the ball in flight.

Pure innocence.

To be clear, innocence does not conflict with confidence. You always want to feel confident when you play. But there is a fine line in the mixture of confidence and innocence to play well. The dynamics of producing fluid motion are exact dynamics. They don't fluctuate and they are not different for different players. These dynamics must be honored.

Why is staying on the couch so important? Here are the dynamics. Ultimately, time controls the muscles. When one experiences time normally, the cerebellum syncs the swing. Time being experienced normally means you are witnessing the swing unfold as it physically unfolds and not over-anticipating anything happening until it actually happens. When time is experienced as distorted, meaning you are over-anticipating an action that has not yet occurred, the swing has less of a chance of being synced correctly. So, let's say you are the top of your swing, and start over-anticipating the result of the shot, so you are "off the couch" in a manner of speaking, and chances are you will get a little quick up there and the transition may not be smooth. At the top, you were in the future. Time was distorted.

A question that may help clarify this is: Do you attack good rounds or do good rounds find you?

They find you. And quite often they find you unexpectedly. On tour, think of how many players shoot themselves out of the tournament by the third round, and then post a low number in the final round. This happens often. Think of your own rounds, when you were expecting to play well that day, and then started out missing shots so you figured it's not going to be your day. You more or less give up and then start to light it up. Why?

You stayed on the couch. You were not too sure who was coming to your dinner party and as a result, guess who showed up? The combination of people (and shots!) you were hoping for. It could be somewhat of an unsettling feeling when you are driving to the course to play and you do not know what is going to show up that day. We always want to feel like we are in control of our own destiny; that we are the captains of our own ship. But you must, and I repeat, you must, honor and pay homage to the laws of nature that sync the swing and produce fluid motion. You cannot be a bull in a china shop and demand excellence. It just doesn't work like that.

The FC is very simple in regard to the dinner party story. Start hitting balls and after each shot ask yourself whether you were on the couch or off the couch. This sounds very abstract but after the first shot you will know whether you were on or off it. It's a distinct feeling when either occurs. It feels like a surprise when you hit one being on the couch. That is because when you are on the couch, you have not over-anticipated the shot turning out exactly as you planned.

This is in contrast to being off the couch, when you did over-anticipate an action that has not yet occurred. When this over-anticipatory dynamic is set up, immediately after you hit a shot, to free the mind, the mind has to compare when you over-anticipated to what actually occurred. As a result of this comparison, often the body loses its balance. And there is no surprise as to the outcome, because in a way you have already hit the shot twice; once in your over-anticipatory response, usually at the transition, and second, the actual hitting of the shot.

Because you have hit the shot twice (and probably

even more times mentally), there is no feeling of surprise when you see how it turned out. And for sure there is no feeling of innocence during the whole process. But when there is no over-anticipatory dynamic set up, either before or during the shot, then when you observe how the shot turned out, there is almost a childlike wonder when you see how well you hit it. You are actually hitting the ball for the first time and not the second time, as when you set-up that over-anticipating sequence of events.

This is not in conflict at all with visualization. You must visualize a shot to hit it. The problem occurs when you are actually hitting it, not before, when you are visualizing it. The problem occurs in the mind when you are hitting it mentally during the motion, because you are off the couch.

Though it may appear that players competing and winning in tournaments have that totally focused, determined, I-am-going-to-get-this-done-at-any-cost kind of mentality, no-pain-no-gain kind of feelings, the real magic shows up when they are living in the opposite universe: *I am going to feel like a child out there and the golf course is going to be like a sandbox, as I blissfully play away.* Again, think of the deeper meaning of Tiger's quote.

Wandering in the Wilderness

One of the main reasons players get away from naturally Setting One is they find something that works, and then they hold on to it for dear life. They either hold on to a swing thought or to the feeling associated with executing the swing thought successfully. Then the ride gets slippery. The mind is always looking for patterns and when it finds one, it tends to hold on to it. When you find something that works out there, immediately the mind attaches it to it and feels it figured something out, and often, it feels like it figured everything out.

Often though, that which worked beautifully yesterday, completely lets you down today. You recall, it's the 65-75 syndrome. A player shoots a 65, thinks he figured it out and then proceeds to shoot a 75 the next day. When he shot the 65, whatever allowed him to go low that day, became the star of the show the next day and hence his much higher score. One can say that he went against a fundamental aspect of how the mind likes to operate when producing fluid motion and that is the concept of chunking.

When learning or producing motion, the mind likes to chunk elements of the movement. Meaning if you get too specific with something and isolate it from the environment around it, it weakens the ability to sync the motion. For example, let's say someone that shot the 65 we were just talking about, felt they shot it because they have been working getting the club in a certain position at the top of the swing. The felt they got the club in that position in the majority of shots when they shot a 65.

The next day, thinking the reason for the 65 the previous day was built around where the hands were at the top of the swing, they put a lot of attention in getting their hands in that same position. That goes in the opposite direction of chunking information. They are now living in the world of specificity. The result?

Timing becomes compromised. The reason they had success the day before was they were able to put their attention on where they wanted the hands to be at the top of the swing **and** for whatever reason, chunk that attention with the elements of the swing that occurred immediately before and immediately after. It broke down the next day because they were unable to do that. Wholeness was broken.

The same sequence happens with regard to holding on to a certain feeling. Let's say someone plays very well, analyzes their round and remembers they had a certain feeling out there. And let's say that feeling was associated with how they felt at the top of their swing. Of course, everyone wants to hold on to something that works, so the next day their primary goal is to replicate that feeling at the top of the swing. The result?

They don't play well at all. Not only does the mind like to chunk positions in a golf swing, it also likes to chunk feelings. That means if you try to isolate one feeling rather than experiencing feelings in a holistic environment, you risk shutting down the cerebellum's ability to sync the swing. If you try to look for some security blanket out there, something you feel will make the round work that day, you may be disappointed more times than not. Then what should you be holding on to out there? What should your goal be? One word.

Wholeness.

You can't say that word enough. The brain physiology loves wholeness and you will play your best when you consistently experience it. If you chase the by-products of experiencing wholeness, successfully executing a swing thought or holding on to a feeling too tightly, most likely you will not play your best that day and in the long run, may not reach your potential as a golfer.

Fluid Motion Factor Checklist

The final piece of information in the second set of Fluid Cues is the checklist.

Where do you go when you miss a shot? Typically, the only place players go is the swing. After all, something happened in the swing or else they would have hit a good shot. On one level, that makes perfect sense. Something had to happen in the swing. That is unquestionable. The real question is not that it happened, **but why it happened**. That is the more fundamental question.

Muscle memory does not break down. Not week by week and certainly not swing by swing. Let's assume a player has a repeatable swing, meaning they have enough money in the bank that when they go the range and hit a bucket of balls, most of the time, they are hitting the ball just fine. This player is now on the course and has just missed a shot. Really missed it.

Immediately, they start analyzing what went wrong in their swing. Maybe they felt they took it too far inside (possible), were too quick on the way down (another possibility) or left the clubface open at impact (another possibility), and that is why it went right. Let's say all the above did happen. No argument there. The club was taken too far on the inside, they were too quick on the way down and for sure, they left the clubface open at impact.

The traditional way to fix this on the next shot is to put some attention on not doing the above things. But remember, muscle memory does not break down. What if every time you missed a shot, you could drop a ball and hit another shot? Or even another shot.

Eventually, on the second or third shot you would hit a good one. So if there were something really mechanically wrong with your swing, regardless of how many balls you dropped and hit after that missed first shot, you would be hard pressed to hit a good shot.

But that is not the case. In fact, it is far from the case. On the second dropped ball, you would most likely hit an acceptable shot. **Once the money is in the bank, it's always in the bank.**

Defaulting to fixing the part of the swing that broke down, is defaulting to the superficial element of the problem. On one level, of course something happened in the swing every time a shot is missed. That's why you missed! But the more fundamental question that should be asked, and answered, is, "Why didn't you access what you already own?" And to answer that question, here is the Fluid Motion Factor checklist. You use this when you miss a shot.

The FMF checklist asks three questions:

1. *Was the algorithm set? If the algorithm was not set, it would be difficult, if not impossible, to Set One. You can only Set One, experiencing wholeness before you pull the trigger, if*

the algorithm has been firmly established. If it hasn't, the different parts of the shot, such as the lie or the shape, will be pulsating around in your mind over the ball, not connected to each other, and wholeness will be broken. It's like you want to make a smoothie and all the ingredients are in the container, but you never hit the blend button and you still try to drink it. It comes out a mess when you pour it into a glass.

2. *Let's assume the algorithm was set. You knew exactly what you wanted to do. Then you ask yourself the second question in the checklist: Was there a threshold level of wholeness before you pulled the trigger? In other words, was One set? If One was not set before you pulled the trigger, then why in the world would you be surprised you missed the shot? You shouldn't.If wholeness is not experienced before you pull the trigger, chances are wholeness will not be experienced during the shot. The two go hand in hand. If wholeness was not established before the shot, then ask yourself the question, "What broke wholeness?" Something specific broke wholeness. It could be the lie felt different from what you thought it would be when you set the algorithm, the consequences of hitting a good or bad shot started to pulsate, and/or you started to question something about how you wanted to hit*

*the shot. **Something** started to pulsate or wholeness would not have been broken. You first acknowledge that One was not set and then you determine the cause of why it was not set.*

3. *But let's say the algorithm was set, One was set, and you still missed the shot. You then ask yourself, "What broke wholeness during the swing?" Something broke wholeness during the swing or you would have hit an acceptable shot. Once you ask yourself this question, you will know what broke it. It could have been a swing thought, trying to get it close to the pin or hit the fairway, or the ramification of making or missing the putt, or any number of other things, but for sure, something broke wholeness or chances are you would have hit an acceptable shot. If you really cannot figure out what broke wholeness, which should only be rarely if you are honest with yourself, then most likely the target broke wholeness, because we are always trying to get it close to the target.*

Asking yourself these three questions will allow you to understand, from a fundamental level, why you missed the shot. Of course, if someone took a video of your swing, something is going to show up that caused the miss. Obviously. But the point is to not dance around the issue and become a prisoner of the surface level of the problem. If you do that, you will always be practicing the surface level of the solution. This is another reason why golfers fail to reach their potential. They are not practicing solving their poor swings from a fundamental level.

The FMF checklist forces you to address the miss from a fundamental level and it gives you a better chance to re-set the clock on the next shot. For instance, let's say you just missed your drive to the left. You analyze the miss from the perspective of the swing and you conclude that you pulled it, so on the next shot or at least on the next drive, you put your attention on not pulling it by swinging out to the target, rather than pulling your follow-through across your body. In your mind, this is how the problem will be fixed.

Successfully Putting Your Attention on a Part

By putting your attention on doing something specific during the swing, often you will not Set One and therefore will not experience a threshold level of wholeness during the swing.

There is an exception to this, but it becomes a delicate tightrope to walk. Let's say you know when you are not swinging well, you lift the club up, rather than dragging it back. Keep in mind though, that when you are doing that, it's a byproduct of violating some rule of the bank. On the range, or playing a practice round, that does not occur. Keep that in mind because it is a very important point.

So, you put your attention on not lifting, but dragging the club back and, lo and behold, you start hitting the ball well again. Let's say there is another player that has the same issue and he also tries to fix it by putting his attention on the same part of the swing: drag it back, rather than lift it. This golfer does not fix the problem. In fact, he exacerbates it and his swing becomes less effective. Why the different results using the same solution?

Simple. The golfer who was able to fix the problem was successful because wholeness was not broken while putting their attention on a part. The golfer that was not successful broke wholeness by putting too much attention on a part. He could not put his attention on a part and still experience a threshold level of wholeness.

It's a very cut-and-dried situation. Some golfers are able to put their attention on a part of the swing and not break wholeness, while for others, wholeness is broken when this occurs.

Those who are successful in putting their attention on a part while not breaking wholeness are rare. But what choice do they really have when their swing starts to break down? They only have Plan A: Try to fix the swing. But in reality, there is really nothing wrong with their swing. They have violated a rule of the bank and as a result, did not have access to their rightful, hard-earned money.

There is a better plan. Plan B. It is not my plan; it is everyone's plan that has a repeatable motion. It is understanding which rule of the bank was violated so you have a better chance of not violating it the next shot. This is where the FMF checklist comes in. Ninety percent of the time it will explain why you missed the shot from the most fundamental perspective. This program always wants to take you to the root of the problem and not dance around surface explanations. Always when you miss, something happened in the swing, that is obvious, but you want to answer the more important question of why it happened.

When you have gone through all the Setting One FCs and picked one you felt most comfortable with, evaluate your misses using the FMF checklist. If it pops up in your mind that you did this or that with the club, fine; just acknowledge it without thinking about it in too much detail. If you played enough, you know your swing and you know what happens when you don't make a good swing, so keep the drama to a minimum. It's time to solve the problem, rather than drown in the misery.

FMF Scorecard

While we are talking about evaluating misses from more fundamental levels, let's talk about evaluating your play from more fundamental levels. The evaluative criteria you use when practicing is crucial in the success of using the FMF program. This will become clearer in the third and fourth set of FCs, but let's talk about using different evaluative criteria when playing. Your score is the normal evaluative criteria when playing. You may also be using GIR or how many putts per round or any of a variety of other stats to see how you are doing out there.

Let's introduce another set of evaluative criteria. The FMF scorecard. The FMF scorecard evaluates why you hit a lot of fairways and greens or sank a lot of putts. Here's how it works.

You are going to give yourself one number on each shot, based on the average of adding two indexes together—how much wholeness you had before you started the swing and how much wholeness you had during the swing.

> **Give yourself a one when you had a lot of wholeness, a two when there was a medium amount, and a three when there was little wholeness.**

For instance, let's say on one shot, you Set One well and you give yourself a one. But wholeness was broken during the swing, so you give yourself a two. You add the two numbers together and divide by two, the number of shots. Your score on that hole was a 1.5.

Write down the score for every shot and for every putt. Then at the end of the round, add all the numbers up and divide by the total number of shots and that will be your FMF score for the round. Any score around 1.5 is excellent.

By using abstract criteria to evaluate your round, you are culturing the mind to experience more and more abstraction. Abstraction is the same as wholeness. I will talk about that in the next set of Fluid Cues. When you had your best rounds, you experienced more wholeness before and during the shot than when you had your most challenging rounds. Practicing something that will begin to culture the mind to experience what it has to experience when playing your best, instead of it just showing up by chance, is practicing with purpose.

The Second Set of Fluid Cues—Review

1. *The mind produces fluid motion when it experiences wholeness.*
2. *Muscle memory does not break down. What breaks down is the ability to access it.*
3. *The target is not really your friend.*
4. *Don't take Universe One into Universe Two.*
5. *Dinner party story.*
6. *Use the FMF checklist:*

Four Setting One Fluid Cues

Nines into the shot, Set One, swing.
Nines into the shot, Set One and then Set One at the top.
Nines into the shot, Set One for the first two or three feet of take-a way.
Nines into the shot, Set One and keep One Set throughout the whole swing.

Target Fluid Cues

From one to five, how much did the target break wholeness at the top of the swing?
Hit a ball to a target and then to no target and see if there was a difference in the swing.

Were you on or off the couch?

The main goal of the second set of fluid cues is to show the importance of experiencing wholeness during the swing. The brain physiology creates a fluid swing when it experiences a threshold level of wholeness during a motion.

4

The Gap

The Zone experience I had in 1975 that led to the writing of this book occurred on a tennis court. It was the experience that led to a 45-year life journey of understanding how fluid motion is produced in every sport. If I didn't have that experience, that journey might not have occurred and this book would never have been written. I thought it would be interesting to explain what happened on that memorable day on the court.

When you watch a tennis match, what do you see? One person hits a ball and then the other person hits a ball. This continues until someone wins the point. So, you can define tennis as a series of shots, or a series of motions.

What else is happening? One person hits the ball and waits. Then the other person hits the ball and waits. So, if you switch your attention from the person who is hitting to the person who is waiting, you can define tennis as a series of waitings, or a series of gaps. Though this is obviously not what you would do when watching a match, nevertheless it is occurring. As it turns out, the quality of these waitings, or gaps, will determine the quality of the shot.

Here's how it works. Time controls the muscles. If there is an imbalance in the gap, meaning time is experienced as moving quickly, that imbalance will immediately show up in the stroke. It's like there are two columns, A and B. A is the gap, B is the motion. B will always be a byproduct of A. By the time you initiate the motion, it's too late. The shot will form according to what is experienced in the gap. A structures B.

Here is the example that all tennis players have had that proves this point. Let's say you are returning serve, and your opponent hits a serve that is two inches out. You proceed to hit the best return of the day. But of course, it doesn't count, because it is out.

He then hits a second serve that is two inches in and you proceed to hit your typical, off the back-foot, semi-defensive, just-get-the-ball-in return. Why the difference in returns? And not with the obvious surface level explanations that one ball was in and the other out.

Between the time the service ball bounces and is returned, there is a gap. If the ball is traveling at 100 mph, the gap is about 1/10th of a second, but nevertheless it's a gap. The difference in the two returns is how that gap was experienced. On the first serve that was out, the player experienced the gap without time being distorted. On the second serve that was in, there was a slight distortion of time because they realized the point had to be played, so there was a slight over-anticipatory response created.

The difference in returns was due to how that 1/10th of a second was experienced.

My Zone experience was due to how I experienced the gap. On that day, for whatever reason, because I never even thought about the concept of a gap, I experienced the gap differently from how I had ever experienced it in my life. Time stood still. I had all the time in the world to do whatever and whenever I wanted with the ball and it felt effortless, and even blissful to do so. While waiting for the ball, I was living in an ocean of silence. Afterwards, it honestly felt like the Higher Forces in Nature had given me a gift.

Because the reason for my extraordinary play that day was subtle and under the radar, it took me a few days to understand what happened. But when it did dawn on me, my understanding of tennis and eventually all sports was turned upside down.

Every player and every instructor is only focused on the motion. If you are a beginner in any sport, you have to learn correct mechanics. But there comes a point in time when the motion is grooved, where it is mechanically sound and at that point, it is all about performance. The common understanding is that performance will improve when the motion **gets even better than it is now**. So, what's the eternal game plan? Eternally continue working on the motion.

That could lead to swing prison, the focus of Chapter 8. I realized with the experience I had, that the focus in playing and instruction, at a certain point in time in a player's career, had to undergo a radical transformation. For players to reach their potential in the game or give themselves the best chance to have those magical Zone experiences, non-motion had to take priority, as well as the processes in the mind during that non-motion, that produce fluid motion. There are specific processes in the mind that must be experienced in the gap in order for the motion to unfold successfully.

Think about a golf swing. If you define a gap as where there is no motion, there are three gaps: address, transition, (the body may not stop moving, but the club does), and the end of the swing. These are the three crucial points in a motion. These pauses will more or less determine the quality of the shot for an accomplished player. There is just too much club-head speed created in a golf swing to micro-manage what is going on. Gaps will determine the quality of the motion, especially the gap before you pull the trigger. At that point you are creating the blueprint for the shot. And most create a complicated, over-focused based blueprint and then of course, by the time they pull the trigger, it's too late.

The importance of gaps is found in many different areas of life. Think of the gap between notes in music. What distinguishes musical geniuses is how they handle that space. Someone listening to a Heifetz or Perlman, if they are an accomplished musician, within 10 or 15 seconds can recognize they are listening to a musical genius. Think of the gaps between words in a talented actor or actress. It's called timing and they have it down perfectly. Or think of your own speech when you want to make a point in a conversation. Your pauses will often get the point across often more strongly than your actual words.

Even in nature, gaps are significant. An atom is mostly empty space. It has electrons circulating around it and a nucleus at its center. How much empty space is there in an atom? 99.99999999996% empty space! Let's put in this way: If a hydrogen atom were the size of the earth, the proton at its center would be 600 feet across.

And nature loves simplicity, hence the name of this book. One of the most universal laws of nature in the universe is the law of least action. Nature likes to choose the path of least resistance and likes to economize all Her actions, whether it be the path a light beam travels between two mirrors or the path an apple takes when it drops from a tree. It is no different in the mind. When someone plays their best, they feel like they are not doing much at all, as if everything is happening automatically and effortlessly.

This also has to do with the third law of thermodynamics and the vacuum state. The third law states that if you reduce the activity of a system, you increase the orderliness. For instance, when we freeze water, we are reducing the activity in the water so that eventually it freezes and becomes more orderly. An ice cube is more orderly than a glass of water.

The vacuum state of a field is the state of least excitation of that field. It is the most orderly and most powerful state of that field. When you access the Fluid

Motion Factor, you access the most powerful state of the mind, the state where fluid motion is produced. When that happens, it never feels like you are doing much when you play because the mind is operating from its most powerful level with the eyes open; you can say it is operating from its vacuum state. When you imitate how nature functions, you become more powerful, more coherent, more successful. Creating motion from the vacuum state of the mind is the hallmark of all the great athletes in the world, regardless of the sport.

When the mind is deeply settled during a motion, it produces alpha waves, which are associated with Zone experiences. Alpha waves can only be produced when the mind experiences non-specificity. Non-specificity means the mind has awareness, but awareness of nothing specific. A secular definition of non-specificity would be making a golf smoothie, where no aspect of the shot is pulsating over any other aspect. When there is too much specificity, meaning you did not make a smoothie and something is pulsating about the swing or the shot, the mind produces beta waves, which tend to compromise the cerebellum's ability to sync a swing.

With this insight of the gap I experienced 45 years ago, I set out to take care of these gaps and develop a program that effortlessly and consistently allowed someone to experience them in a certain way. I wanted to develop a program where it felt like less and less was happening in these gaps, until it felt like nothing was happening at all. This was a subtle journey for me. The body was about to go into motion, or during the motion make a significant transition, and you always want to give it the best chance to produce an effective motion. This is done by taking care of the gaps. It is a 180-degree shift in priorities for players and coaches. It is understanding non-motion to be the critical moment in every motion.

That is a huge paradigm shift. Essentially, this book is all about gaps.

5

The Third Set of Fluid Cues

The third set of FCs has an interesting origin.

When I was senior in college, in my spring semester, I had completed all my courses for my major so I could take any course I desired. Talk about having a feeling of freedom! I had one more semester left in college to try to become "educated" so I wanted to make the most of it. After some reflection, I thought I should take a music and art course, because after all, music and art form such a substantial part of Western culture.

I took a music course and thoroughly enjoyed it. We studied the usual suspects: Beethoven, Mozart and Bach. But then I took an art course and I fell in love with the study of art. It was a survey course, from fifteenth century to modern art. When we arrived at modern art, the teacher had us buy a book called *Other Criteria* by Leo Steinberg (University of Chicago Press). I had no idea what the book was about, but I immediately felt drawn to the name. At an early age I was an out-of-the-box-thinker and I felt this book was heading in that direction.

I was right. *Other Criteria* eventually became a seminal book in the study of art. Its premise was simple. When you are studying Michelangelo, DaVinci, Caravaggio, or Reubens, you cannot use the same criteria in evaluating their paintings, as when you are studying Picasso, Braque, or Jackson Pollack. Often, when looking at modern art, you are challenged to even understand what you are looking at! In short, you have to use different criteria when studying modern art versus pre-impressionistic art. You have to use other criteria.

We are going to use other criteria in evaluating a golf swing. We are not going to use the standard criteria: strike, direction, distance, tempo, balance, and other traditional measures. We are going to use what I call levels of abstraction.

The mind loves operating from a state of abstraction to produce motion. I consider wholeness and abstraction to be two terms defining the same state, with abstraction, well, being a little more abstract.

Let's revisit Setting One. Setting One refers to the situation where, right before you swing, if you dropped the club, you would feel more or less the same as you would when the club was in your hands and you were about to swing.

Think about this for a moment. You are at the moment of truth; you are about to initiate the swing. Everything about that situation wants to move you away from experiencing wholeness and abstraction to moving towards being concrete, the opposite of being abstract. You could be:

1. *Thinking about the consequences of hitting a good or bad shot*
2. *Thinking about what happened on the last shot you missed*
3. *Thinking about what you need to do in the swing in order to hit a good shot*
4. *Thinking about why you missed the last cut*
5. *Thinking about why the player you grew up with is on tour and you haven't made it out of Stage 1*
6. *Or thinking about many, many, many other things. Not even golf related*

The list is endless. Golf is a brutal sport. You only get one shot. You don't get a second serve. This shot could make or break your round. Or your career. Everything about the situation wants to take you far away from experiencing abstraction and move you to being concrete. It wants you to live in checklist city, a place where you really don't want to be too firmly entrenched.

With all the drama surrounding just about every shot out there, the situation wants to strongly pull you in the direction of being concrete. But, if the mind does not experience a threshold level of wholeness and abstraction before you pull the trigger, it is potentially gambling. In other words, you may not be too sure of what you will get. If you are thinking too much, for instance—of too many elements of the shot using **concrete criteria**—then wholeness will probably be broken and indeed you are at the poker table at the Bellagio.

Remember, the swing does not control the swing. Processes in the mind control the swing. So, one has to give unto Caesar, what is due to Caesar. All golfers should learn how to access the processes in the mind that allow for good tempo and balance when they are the learning the grip, set-up and other fundamental elements of the game. Perhaps this is the most fundamental element they can learn because it controls every aspect of the swing.

The body has no intelligence to ititiate a swing. You can't read this sentence enough times. The intelligence in the body flows from the mind. Being completely familiar with and honoring the environment the mind has to operate from in order to produce fluid motion will greatly increase the chances of producing fluid motion. That is why these levels of abstraction in Fluid Cues are so powerful.

Here's how they work.

Take a full swing without a ball. Evaluate the swing based on your level of anticipation. By level of anticipation, I am referring to how much anticipation you had in hitting a good shot, or swinging well or having good tempo, or any criteria you wish to use. Obviously, this is a practice swing, so you are not hitting anything, but imagine this would be your normal swing when you do hit a ball. No phony baloney. Go after it.

After each swing give yourself a number from one to ten on how much anticipation you had. One means you had very little anticipation and ten means you had a great deal of it. Take as many practice swings as needed to arrive at a one or two level. You will probably start off around a five or six, which is normal, but keep swinging away until you experience what a one or two feels like. In other words, you are setting a baseline.

After you set a baseline of what a one or a two feels like, you are going to hit a ball. **But** you are not going to use the traditional criteria of evaluating a shot: strike, direction, distance, tempo or any other kind of concrete criteria. You are going to use abstract criteria to evaluate the shot. This means that the traditional criteria of strike, direction, and so on are completely irrelevant. I know that sounds radical but just stay with me here and I will explain why using abstract criteria is so powerful.

When you use concrete criteria, which virtu-ally everyone does on every shot, by definition, you are culturing the mind to be concrete. For instance, let's say you are working on getting the club at the top in a certain position. When you do get the club in that position, you are satisfied, and when you do not, you are not. The criterion is concrete and simple. You practice this way all week long, or maybe all month long and then you tee it up at a big tournament.

Here's the kicker. The only way you are going to consistently get the club in the right position at the top is **if the mind is abstract**. Remember, abstraction and wholeness define the same experience. Yet, you have just hit 1000 or 2000 balls with the mind being concrete on every shot. You have just spent the whole time on the range specifically doing that.

> **The mind is weakened when it is concrete and strengthened when it is abstract.**

Knowing that, why would you think if you just spent many hours using concrete evaluative criteria on every swing, that you can just switch gears on that first tee and have the mind become abstract?

Usually you can't. You are just hoping and praying that you can. Vegas.

If you practiced the whole week culturing the mind to be abstract, however, it starts to be your default state and then you have a much better chance of having the mind abstract when you do tee it up. Now this goes against just about every teaching philosophy you have ever come across. In order to work on your swing you do have to put your attention on it and practice it diligently. My response? Yes and no. Of course, you have to put your attention on something in order to change it, but what exactly should your attention be on? Key question.

Unless a teacher or player can answer one fundamental question, they will always be searching for the answer as to how they will improve. The question is simple: **How is fluid motion produced and why does it break down?** That's it. And unless everything you do when you practice and when you play is connected to answering that question, you may have a permanent seat at the blackjack table.

So even when practicing something in your swing,

you first have to connect that practice with answering the above question. I will talk later in the book on how to make changes or practice your swing using the principles of FMF, but for now, just remind yourself on a deeper, softer level of the mind to do essentially something you already know how to do—getting the club in the right position at the top.

To transform intention into execution, the mind has to experience wholeness, it has to experience abstraction. This is what this book is all about: how to transfer intention into execution. The traditional understanding is that you just practice until you can do it on demand. In other words, you practice and practice and then you practice some more until you get it right.

Practice is important but if it were the determining factor on any tour, the players who practiced the most would always make it. But this is far from the case. Don't get me wrong. Practice is crucial to make it in any professional sport. The point being raised here is this: Just what should be the priority when you practice? I will answer that question in the next chapter.

Let's return to our first level of abstraction Fluid Cue. Once you have established a baseline of what a low level of anticipation feels like (**low level of anticipation equates to high level of abstraction**), then you are going to hit a ball. But you are not going to use the standard criteria in evaluating the shot. What are the standard criteria? Strike, direction, tempo, balance, positions, and so on. All of those criteria do not matter!

You are going to use one and only one criterion

for evaluating the shot: your level of anticipation. This means regardless of how you hit the ball, or to stretch it to its limits, **if you hit the ball!**, the only criterion available is your level of anticipation, whether before the swing, during, or a combination of both.

Your level of anticipation will probably start at a five or a six. This is normal. Be self-disciplined and only use your level of anticipation to evaluate the shot. Eventually you will notice that your level of anticipation will go lower. You should also observe that as the level of anticipation number decreases (again, which means level of abstraction increases), the shots become better. You need to hit as many balls as necessary to see this correlation. Take your time, but this correlation needs to be seen.

Once you have seen this correlation, it is time to take a major step into a new golfing universe—a simpler, less complex, more repeatable universe that will give you a better chance of playing consistent golf and reaching your potential in the game. The paradigm shift is:

The more abstract your criteria are in evaluating a shot, the better chance you have of accessing the Fluid Motion Factor. Conversely, the more concrete your evaluation is, the less chance you have of accessing the Fluid Motion Factor.

Though the implications of this statement have not been discussed on the Golf Channel, it is just a matter of time until they are. The next advancement in golf instruction will not be about equipment or technology. The next advancement, and it will be a huge advancement, is the understanding of how fluid motion is produced in a golf swing, why it breaks down, and techniques to make the mind access that fluidity more consistently.

If it is true, which it is, that the mind operates best when it is soaked in abstraction, why aren't golfers culturing the mind to be abstract during practice? Which begs the question: How do golfers practice?

Exactly the opposite!

Pardon the shouting, but in my opinion, this is the main reason why the game is not growing, why players do not reach their potential and why people quit the game. Go to any driving range in the country (or the world) and what do you see? You see what I call a report-card mentality. That means on every shot, golfers gives themselves a grade… "I hit the target, that's an A." "I missed the target; that's a C." "I got it close, that's a B+."

When you use concrete criteria to evaluate every shot, you are culturing the mind to be concrete. Using concrete criteria always translates into culturing the mind to be concrete. Using concrete criteria weakens the mind.

Consider this: You have a big tournament coming up. You want to play well, so you want your practice sessions to count. Every ball should count. So, every time you hit a ball you are sure to give yourself a grade on it. Close to the target, A, not close, C, and so on. You hit close to a thousand balls that week. Every shot a grade!

Now, what have you just done? The mind, as you now know, is weakened when it is concrete. When the mind is concrete it is:

1. *Challenging to have good tempo*
2. *Challenging to have good balance*
3. *Challenging to sync the swing*
4. *Challenging to control the distance on your wedges and putts*

You get the picture.

So, are you practicing culturing the mind to be abstract or concrete when you practice? That's obvious. If you spend hours and hours culturing the mind to be concrete and then you step on the first tee and the only way you can play consistent golf is if the mind is abstract, why would you be surprised you are not improving? Or perhaps even moving in the opposite direction?

You shouldn't be surprised. It is like studying French for many years and then you decide not to go to France, but China. You can't speak the French you learned when you're in China. When using concrete criteria on every shot, you are simply culturing something that will usually prevent you from playing your best. Essentially, you are just hoping and praying that your mind can be in abstract mode when you tee it up in that tournament, because you surely did not have a systematic plan to have that occur.

If fluid motion is produced when the mind is abstract and not produced when the mind is concrete, then shouldn't your practice sessions be set up so that you are culturing the mind to be abstract?

Exactly.

Now, back to the abstract Fluid Cues. Once you have seen the correlation between level of acceptance and quality of shot, **and you need be absolutely convinced of this**, you should have enough of a subjective experience to change your paradigm. Once that occurs, you are in a different universe.

You are systematically practicing what the mind needs to experience to play consistently. Your practice will now be tied directly to what has to occur in order to play well in that big tournament of yours. No more hoping and wishing that the mind becomes abstract on that first tee. You have a plan.

I am going to give you further instruction on how to do these abstract Fluid Cues. The mere fact that you are using abstract criteria to evaluate the shot is good enough. You don't have to quantify the results. You don't try to have a low level of anticipation. In fact, it doesn't matter what level of anticipation you do have.

The key phrase when you are hitting balls, in terms of level of anticipation, is "passive observer" rather than active participant. The analogy is that you just spent two hours cleaning your room and as you are walking out the door, you just take a quick glance to see how everything looks. Just a quick look. No homing in at any part of the room. That's what passive observer means. So, don't give yourself a number.

When using abstract criteria to evaluate a shot, you are clearing the path to the basal ganglia to access your best swings. You are making the path to the basal ganglia to be like the autobahn. You are culturing the mind to become more and more familiar with the state of mind that leads to consistency. When using concrete criteria, you are culturing the mind to be concrete, the opposite state it needs to be in order to play consistent golf.

Back to the Abstract Fluid Cues. I would suggest hitting 20 or 30 balls using each one. Here are they are:

1. *Anticipation*
2. *Concern*
3. *Expectation*
4. *Intensity of intention (how intense was your intention to hit a good shot or swing well or hit your target or whatever else you want to do with the shot)*
5. *Anxiety*
6. *Fear*
7. *Peace (high is good)*
8. *Love (often there is not a lot of love in your shot! High is good)*

With each one of these, establish a baseline first without a ball. Swing as many times as needed to get to a one or two. Then and only then, start hitting a ball. And don't pay attention to what number you had on each shot. Again, the fact that you are using abstract criteria is good enough to be moving the mind toward abstraction.

Though all the above are different threads of abstraction, they have the same goal: culturing the mind to be more and more familiar with a state of abstraction.

Tiger was living in the world of pure abstraction during times like this: "There are many putts or many shots where I don't remember hitting. I remember seeing the ball flight. I remember preparing for the shot, pulling the club out of the bag, and once I'm behind the ball, I'm walking into the shot and I don't remember until I see the ball leave."

When Bubba said, "I didn't remember anything about the last nine holes" in the 2013 Masters, he was living in the world of pure abstraction.

And when Maria Sharapova admitted she had no idea how she beat Serena Williams in the finals of Wimbledon, she was living in the world of pure abstraction.

If this is the case in all three examples and in countless others, wouldn't it be an excellent plan to systematically culture the mind to experience abstraction as one of the main goals in your practice?

Just a quick note. When working with someone who won a major championship, he told me he would never win again on tour unless his mind became more abstract. Many pros, though not able to express it as succinctly as that, I am sure, feel the same way. They had success out there and then started to work nonstop on their swing. They won because they were abstract. It's the only way you can win. Then they dove into being as concrete as possible, moving more and more in the direction of being in swing prison. Many ended up never winning again.

The Third Set of Fluid Cues—Review

The mind loves abstraction. When using abstract criteria to evaluate shots, it is strengthened and when using concrete criteria, is weakened.

Set a baseline of 1 to 10 with each level of abstraction. When you establish that baseline, hit balls only using that level of abstraction as your criteria in evaluating the shot.

6

The Fourth Set of Fluid Cues

Time to break out the champagne and caviar. The fourth set of Fluid Cues is being served.

When someone stands behind the ball and sets up their shot, they visualize it. Even if this visualization doesn't take place on the surface level of the mind, nevertheless it takes place somewhere in the mind, because it is virtually impossible to hit a golf shot without some sort of visualization.

When you visualize the shot, obviously you do not visualize the shot going right or left of your target, or long or shot of your target, but visualize it going exactly where you want it to go. The problem occurs, and it is a big problem, when you have a very low level of acceptance as to the outcome of the shot.

We are venturing into a subtle arena here. Of course you want the shot to go exactly where you want it to go. Why would you want it to go anywhere but there and why would you even think it is a good idea if it went anywhere else? You wouldn't. But when the level of acceptance is too low, then two unfortunate circumstances can occur during the swing.

If the level of acceptance is too low, meaning **it has to go exactly where you want it to go and you cannot accept any other option**, you are giving a green light for the PFC to go online and get involved in the motion. Remember, the PFC is the killer in a golf swing. The main goal in a golf swing is to keep the PFC offline. If you have done that, you have an excellent chance of hitting an acceptable shot.

But the nature of the PFC, like a CEO in a company, wants to get involved in every aspect of the motion. In fact, it's just standing on the sidelines waiting to get involved. With a very low level of acceptance, you are sending it a handwritten invitation. Here's how.

When you have a low level of acceptance during the swing, and usually at the transition, the PFC goes online to see if what you are doing will result in what you wanted to do. This is subtle. Because your level of acceptance is so low (my way or the highway!), the PFC says to itself, "Fine, I hear you loud and clear, let's just see if what is occurring during the swing will result in what you expected."

It then goes online and compares what you anticipated to what is currently happening, and in that comparison, the loops are broken, and the cerebellum is challenged to sync the swing.

In a way, this is a somewhat counter-intuitive understanding for most, because one is taught that when you do put your attention on something, you have a better chance of executing. In other words, by putting your attention on where the club should be, or where you want the ball to go, you have a better chance of successfully executing it.

That may be true to a certain extent, but on too many occasions you may win the battle and lose the war. You may indeed get the club in the right position, but in so doing wholeness is broken and the cerebellum fails to sync the other parts of the swing. I think you understand by now, that too much attention on anything will tend to break wholeness.

Attention does not necessarily equate to execution. That is a crucial concept to understand. Just because you put your attention on something during the swing, does not mean you will be successful in executing it. Holistic attention is the determining factor in what gets the job done. This means when you put your attention on getting the club in a certain position, you are not making that detail the star of the show and you are still making a smoothie with all the other elements of the shot.

But when you have a low level of acceptance, you are moving in the opposite direction. You are saying, "I have to hit the ball **exactly** where I want to," or "I have to get the club **exactly** where I want it," and that just wakes up the PFC. That low level of acceptance breaks wholeness.

You have experienced this countless times in the second ball syndrome. You are in the middle of the fairway with a perfect lie, and perfect distance for a club and you miss the green. You drop a ball in disgust and you stick it four feet. What was your level of acceptance on the first shot and what was your level of acceptance on the second shot?

Exactly.

Here is the second unfortunate situation that can happen during the swing when you have a low level of acceptance. When you are behind the ball and determine what kind of shot you want to hit, immediately you input all the processes necessary to hit that shot. You have programmed the computer.

You input different processes for different shots. There are different processes inputted for a 30-foot putt versus a cut five-iron. It is similar to what an ATM machine does. You go to an ATM machine, put in your debit card, punch in your PIN, decide on the amount and the ATM gives you money. If you want $20 versus $120, different levers will be activated in the machine.

Once you tell the machine what you want, you do not have to revisit it and remind it that you want $20, rather than $120. It is the same with inputting the processes in the mind for any shot. But when you have a low level of acceptance, then often the following occurs.

Because you have such a low level of acceptance, the PFC goes online during the motion, takes a subset of the algorithm, for instance, "don't hit it left" or "get the club in this position", and in doing so, immediately inputs another set of processes. Then this set of processes competes with the original set of processes and in this competition, the loops are broken and the cerebellum is challenged to sync the swing.

But, if you do something counterintuitive, something you would never think of doing, and that is, on a scale of 1 to 10, with 1 being a low level of acceptance and 10 a high level, before taking one step into the shot, **you have a 10 level of acceptance**. This means you stand behind the ball and you cannot take one step into the shot until you have accepted all possible outcomes of the shot. This idea is more radical than anything that happened in the 1960s!

By accepting all possible outcomes you have a much better chance of keeping the PFC offline. Why? Because it has nothing to "chew" into during the shot because you have accepted all possible outcomes! If you have accepted the shot, this means your PFC has accepted the shot and there is no need for it to:

1. *Either compare what you are doing during the motion to what you anticipated, or*
2. *Input another set of processes during the swing.*

You are free at last!

The argument can be made that since you have accepted all possible outcomes, aren't you opening the door for an undesirable outcome to appear? The answer to this is you will always default to the DNA goal during a motion, regardless of accepting all possible outcomes. The DNA Goal, even if not on the surface level, is always embedded on a deeper level. So, when accepting all outcomes, you will not default to the ball going right or left, but default to the ball going exactly where you wanted it to go. And you have a better chance of it going where you wanted it to go, based on this reasoning.

When you do have a 10 level of acceptance, before you step into the shot (and it may take a while for that to happen), there will always be some kind of physical feeling associated with it. You may feel lighter, or feel the air go out of your lungs or something like that. Then you know you are ready to take your first step.

From a neurophysiological perspective, the counterintuitive Fluid Cue of having a 10 level of acceptance before you take one step into the shot is an excellent strategy for playing consistent golf.

Wholeness Fluid Cue

By now you are familiar with the experience of wholeness. You know what it feels like. Based on that, stand behind the ball, create your algorithm, and you can't take one step into the shot until you have a ten level of wholeness. This may be challenging on difficult shots, because some elements of the shot may be pulsating, and you may need to wait behind the ball longer than usual. But be disciplined.

Once you have a ten level of wholeness, then nines into the shot, Set One, or not Set One, your choice, and pull the trigger.

From Tennis to Golf

Imagine you are playing tennis. You are going to hit four shots in a rally and after the fourth shot, someone will win the point. What normally occurs is that on each shot an umbilical cord is created between the shot you are hitting and the outcome of the shot. Meaning, when you hit the shot, you are connecting that shot, before, during and after, to whether you will win or lose the point.

To be more exact, you are in the middle of the motion, taking the racquet back or bringing the racquet forward or even when you are running to the ball, you are connecting that moment in the motion to an outcome that has not yet occurred: winning or losing the point.

In other words, the shot does not stand on its own integrity. You are always in the future thinking of the consequences of what you are doing. Everything is connected to an outcome that has not yet occurred. While you are in the present hitting the shot, you are also in the future thinking about the outcome.

This is not good. This connectedness prevents you from being in the moment. If at any point in the motion there is an umbilical cord connected to a future event, time will not be experienced normally; it will be experienced as distorted as you are over-anticipating an event that has not yet occurred: winning or losing of the point.

Now switch to golf. The same phenomenon occurs and it occurs all too often, in practice and on the course. During the swing, usually in the transition, often that umbilical cord is created. And it is a very tightly wound cord. What is it connected to?

The target.

At the top of the swing, you are thinking if the shot will result in getting close to the target. At that point in time or at any point in time during the swing, when you are connected to the outcome of the shot, the shot does not stand on its own integrity. It is being evaluated on the basis of something that has not occurred, even if that occurrence is going to happen in a fraction of a second. The drama at the top of the swing can be breathtaking.

A Word about the Transition

I have mentioned a few times about the potential drama in the transition. Here are some specifics as to why that point in the swing is so crucial.

When you create your algorithm, you input all the necessary information to create the shot. It's done. Finished. No need to revisit the algorithm. For the cerebellum, the transition is a crucial place because it is going to review that information momentarily, as the club is about to switch directions. It has to calculate where you are in the swing and prepare for the crucial downward motion. The cerebellum is monitoring the position of the club 100 times per second.

When there is the briefest of pauses in the transition (except for Hideki Matsuyama!), the cerebellum does not want to be disturbed. It wants to do all its calculations in a silent environment. It needs its space. If you input another set of processes at that point because of low acceptance, you are disturbing the environment necessary for the cerebellum to do its job. It's like someone is about to solve a complicated mathematical equation and you ask them if they want to go get a latte at Starbucks.

Experiencing the gap correctly in the transition is crucial for the cerebellum to do its job.

Back to the umbilical cord.

When there is an umbilical cord attached to something in the future, the delicate processes in the mind responsible for syncing the motion are compromised. You are, for that split second, frozen in time and you never want to be frozen in time. You want to experience time flowing like a river, not frozen like a glacier.

Because you only get one shot, everything about playing golf wants to connect you to a future event that has not yet occurred. There is no second serve in golf. The ability to stay disconnected during the swing—**the ability not to connect what you are doing with a future outcome**—determines major championship winners. Remember, the experience of time controls the muscles.

Being disconnected during the swing, however slightly uncomfortable as it initially sounds, and how much it goes against the grain of most instruction, is the goal of the shot. Most golfers have been taught to do the exact opposite; be as connected as possible to the target. In fact, most golfers are taught to be the target! They have been taught to be as connected as they can, because the more connected, the better the chance of hitting the target.

Unequivocally, absolutely, without a doubt, this is wrong. It is wrong from a neurophysiological perspective.

Every teacher and student should be able to answer what I consider the most fundamental question in sports. This is not the first time I have brought this up. The question is, "How is fluid motion produced and why does it shut down?" When I teach the Fluid Motion Factor program, everything is connected to answering that question.

Fluid motion is produced when the brain physiology experiences wholeness during a motion and it shuts down when a part overshadows the whole. This is a very black and white fact and not open for debate. One of the quickest ways to break wholeness is to have the target pulsating at the top of the swing. If you create an umbilical cord to the target at that point in time, you will be rolling the dice on those big cushiony Las Vegas tables.

Let me ask you this. Is the target moving? No. Are you ever going to forget where the target is? No. Then why do you think it is a good idea to have the target pulsating like the lights outside the Bellagio? It is not a good idea. In fact, it is a dangerous idea. But because golfers equate attention with execution, that is, they have been wrongly taught that if they put more attention on something during a swing, whether it be target or positions, they have a better chance of executing. What do they do? They create the strongest possible umbilical cord. And that is dangerous.

Shots are successful when wholeness is experienced. Why would you systematically want to set up the scenario to go in the opposite direction? You shouldn't. The target is always part of the smoothie. If you have a repeatable swing, alignment will dictate where the ball goes, not over-focusing on the target. And since the target is in the smoothie, it will always be softly pulsating in your mind, like all the other elements of the shot. Again, think of the second ball syndrome.

The logical but counterintuitive conclusion is that every time you hit a shot or a putt, you should be culturing the mind to be disconnected to the target, not connected. It's the opposite of what you have been taught and what you may be doing. Many advocate not only being connected to a target, but also picking the smallest target possible, as the smaller the target, the smaller the miss. I am so speechless when I hear this that I have difficulty in responding.

The main goal in practice is to culture being disconnected and abstract on every shot. But of course, we all know the opposite is occurring. When you do create that umbilical cord, you will always be culturing the mind to be concrete. There is a distinct feeling about being connected or disconnected during a shot. Though it may sound abstract, once you have the experience it will be very clear, so here is the path to that experience.

Hit three balls to no target or three putts to no hole. After each shot, ask yourself whether you were connected or disconnected. Once you put your attention on this, you will know immediately whether you were or you weren't. There will be a feeling of ease and freedom when you are disconnected and a feeling of tension and drama when you weren't. After hitting three balls to no target and asking yourself whether you were connected or disconnected, hit a ball to a target and ask yourself the same question.

There are two reasons why you have a target on the fourth shot.

1. *To check your alignment.*
2. *To see if, when you hit to a target, you felt the same way as when you hit to no target.*

Bingo. Now we are talking about making practice highly effective. By hitting balls to no target, you are culturing the mind to be free, to be abstract. That should be the ultimate goal when you play. Why would you have the opposite goal when you practice, that is culturing the mind to be as connected as possible to the target and therefore culturing the mind to be concrete. Is that how you want to feel on the 14th fairway? A feeling of connectedness usually puts you in prison. Think of the second ball syndrome. You are in the middle of the fairway in a practice round with a perfect lie and you miss the green. You drop another ball and knock it three feet. Where was the target on the first shot? Where was the target on the second shot? Were you connected or disconnected on the first shot? The second shot?

Three and One

There is a space between sleeping and waking where you are not really sleeping and you are not really awake. It's a gap of a few seconds at most. Many years ago, when I started developing the Fluid Motion Factor program, I had quite an unusual experience in that gap. It's one of the few times in my life where I felt that I had not generated my thoughts, but that someone had poured them into my head.

This is what was poured into my head: At the end, feel the same as the beginning. It took me a minute or so to put this into the context of a golf swing, but I got it and this Fluid Cue emerged.

We are going to divide the swing into three parts: address is 1, swing is 2, and when you are finished with the swing and there is no more motion, but you haven't come out of it, is 3.

At 3 I want you to feel the same way you felt at 1. Mentally.

Now, it doesn't matter how you felt at 1. You are not trying to feel any specific way. Just be natural. But before you initiate the swing, take a quick snapshot of how you feel. The snapshot should take just a second. Don't extend it or try to hard to remember what that feeling was. In and out, like paparazzi.

And during 2, you are not trying to feel any specific way. Again, just swing and be natural. But at 3, I want you to try to feel the same as you felt at 1.

As in all the Fluid Cues, intention is more important than execution. This means that if you feel or you don't feel the same at 3 as you did at 1, that's fine. In fact, during the swing if you forgot how you felt at 1, that's also fine. Your attention is only on two places during the swing: 1 and 3. Number 2 is irrelevant.

How does this work and why does this work? With this Fluid Cue, you have a specific goal when the swing is done; feel the same at 3 as you did at 1. This is an abstract goal. You are asking yourself to do something abstract at the end of the swing. In order to be abstract at 3, you have to be abstract at 2. You just can't show up at 3 expecting to be abstract without preparing for that. That preparation occurs during 2.

During 2 you must be abstract, but the beauty of the Fluid Cue is you don't have to think about being abstract. It will occur naturally. You are innocently and unconsciously forcing the mind to be abstract at 2 or else there is little or no chance you will be able to achieve the goal of the Fluid Cue. This should free you up and allow the cerebellum to better sync the swing.

Fourth Set of Fluid Cues—Review

1. *Don't take one step into the shot until you have a 10 level of acceptance.*
2. *Don't take one step into the shot until you have a 10 level of wholeness.*
3. *Hit three balls to no target and then one ball to a target and ask yourself if you were connected or disconnected on each shot.*
4. *Divide the swing into three parts: 1 is address, 2 is the motion, and 3 is you are finished with the motion, but haven't come out of the shot. At 3, feel the same way you felt at 1.*

7

Changing a Swing

No one takes up the game of golf and instantly has excellent mechanics. It just doesn't work like that. The golf swing is not the most natural of motions and everyone, including future major championship winners, needs to learn the fundamentals. The question is, what is the quickest and most effective way to teach the swing, and if one has to change a swing, what is the easiest way to do that?

For the most part, teaching someone the swing is a you-did-it or you-didn't-do-it affair. Meaning the teacher tells the student to get the club in a certain position and when they do, the teacher says, "You did it" and when they don't, they say, "You didn't do it."

In my opinion, this is not the most efficient approach and one of the main reasons why golfers don't improve quickly. With the I-did-it/I-didn't-do-it approach, you are not associating making a successful change in the swing, with the processes in the mind that allowed the change to be made.

Making a change in a swing is like a potter trying to mold clay. The first thing a potter does to mold clay is moisten it and make it malleable. Then, when it is placed on the wheel, it is flexible enough that the potter can mold it anyway she wants.

It is the same with swing changes. The first thing that should be done is to make the student's mind malleable. Making it malleable means systematically allowing them to experience a threshold level of wholeness during the swing. By doing that, they are not weakening the processes in the mind responsible for producing fluid motion. Most of the time when making swing changes those processes are compromised because there is so much focus on the swing change, that wholeness is broken.

When the brain is experiencing a threshold level of wholeness, the body becomes liquid. It then has the ability to get into the position that is being worked on. The flow of intelligence between the mind and body is optimum and the players are giving themselves the best chance of quickly making changes.

Here's how it works: The player needs to have and understand the experience of wholeness and its importance in the swing. Without that experience it is not going to work. Let's assume they do have it. Take whatever changes you are trying to make in the swing and ask them to take a practice swing incorporating that change.

But you are going to ask them after they swing how much wholeness they had during the swing, while they were putting their attention on the change. In other words, you are going to use abstract criteria in evaluating the swing. Remember, anytime you use concrete criteria to evaluate something you are culturing the mind to be concrete. Anytime you use abstract criteria, you will be strengthening the mind to be abstract. Because concrete criteria weaken the mind, it is challenging to make swing changes. These are the dynamics.

If you are teaching the you-did-it/you-didn't-do-it approach, the mind is concrete and the most important thing is well…either you did it or you didn't do it. You are making the change the star of the show, not the processes in the mind that allowed you to make the change, the real star of the show.

When working on the range trying to incorporate the change, every swing is a grade on the report card, an "A", a "C", a "B+"—you get the picture. By doing this you are systematically culturing the mind to be concrete. You then go and play and of course all your attention is on the swing change. Every swing you are over-focusing on the swing change and giving yourself a grade on that report card. The result? Hit or miss success and usually frustration. The mistake that was made in this approach was not associating the successful swing that incorporated the swing change, with the processes in the mind that allowed for that successful swing. The slow boat you are sailing just got slower.

Back to the player. She is going to take a practice swing with attention on the swing change and after the swing, give you a number from 1 to 10 on how much wholeness was experienced during the swing. Now we are getting somewhere. We are using abstract criteria to evaluate the swing, which always makes the mind more powerful. And we are associating the successful swing with the processes in the mind that allowed for a successful swing.

Before she can hit a ball, she needs to experience a 9 or 10 level of wholeness in the practice swing. It may take a while to experience this, but both of you must be patient with this. It takes patience because whenever you work on a change in a swing, there is so much attention on the part, that wholeness is usually broken. Practicing having attention on a part without losing a threshold level of wholeness necessary for making the successful change is the key.

Once they experienced a 9 or 10, they can hit a ball. **But you are going to use abstract criteria, not concrete criteria in evaluating the swing.** This means if the swing change happened or it didn't, it is inconsequential. Now that is radical!

The reason why you use abstract criteria in evaluating their swing is when you associate processes in the mind with the successful change, the deposit made in the basal ganglia is more powerful. When you use the I-did-it/I-didn't-do-it approach, it is a weak deposit, because the deposit doesn't take into account the processes in the mind associated with the successful swing. The implications are profound when using this method. The student will make the changes more quickly and when playing, their attention during the swing will be more on abstraction and wholeness, rather than living in their typical report card universe.

Back to the lesson. Even when both of you are using abstract criteria, you will still use concrete evaluation. Both of you will know whether the swing change was there or not there on every shot. But it will be in the background. You must be patient with this strategy, especially the teacher. The teacher has to resist jumping in and using concrete criteria. They have to, in a way, leave their ego at the door.

There is no greater teacher than the cerebellum. The cerebellum is the teaching genius. It teaches children how to walk, ride a bike, throw a ball, and play sports. As an instructor, in my opinion, your primary responsibility is to set up an environment that enlivens the cerebellum. When this occurs,, whatever you are teaching them, the student will learn faster than if you don't activate the cerebellum. When the cerebellum is working properly, the student will start to teach themselves. Defaulting to simpler and more powerful positions will come naturally, even without any awareness that change is happening.

Think of a child learning how to ride a bike. Again, this takes patience for both the teacher and student, but if done properly, it is amazing how quickly changes can be made.

8

Swing Prison

We all have been there; some for life. It's a lonely, lonely place, but with the pot of gold at the end of the rainbow always luring you closer, you feel you have a chance to reach your goal.

"If only I could get my hands in this position, my body in this position, impact in this position." You are living in the world of "if only"—a world of hypothetical possibilities.

But at the end of the day, when you reflect on your game or your career, you think perhaps it would have been wiser to have taken a different path. But then of course, it's too late.

Let's be clear. You have to learn solid fundamentals when learning the game. My suggestion is to search out for the most accomplished and successful teaching professional you can find. Let that pro teach you all they know. Listen carefully. Practice what they teach. But at a certain point, become your own teacher and only see them occasionally to check things like ball and hand position at address and reassurance that all is well in your swing.

My good friend, successful player, and college coach Shelly Liddick highlights this point when she was in college. She was playing well, but one day someone noticed she was constantly working on her swing. Every day, all day. She came up to her and asked, "When will you be done?"

That stopped her dead in her tracks.

When will you be done? That's a poignant question and a question that if answered correctly, could have changed careers. Here are a few stories about that.

There was a very successful player on tour (*very* being highlighted) who was heading for stardom. But he had a quirky move in his swing, a move that no instructor would ever teach. A well-known teacher approached him and said, "If you could correct that move, so your swing is more fundamentally sound, you have a chance to have an extraordinary career."

That player bit the bullet and started working on the change.

He never won again.

Yes, his move was quirky and yes, it would never be taught by a teacher, but he had one thing that held it together and it held it together effectively: timing. Once he lost his timing, he lost his consistency. Working on a part broke wholeness, he could not recover and his career was more or less over.

Here's a longer version of that.

One time, I was giving a presentation at a college coach's camp where high school golfers could meet college golf coaches and perhaps impress then enough for them to offer a scholarship. After my presentation on how fluid motion is produced and why it breaks down, a woman approached me, introduced herself and said, "You don't know me but my name is Angela Torch (not her real name), and my son Anthony (not his real name) is one of the top junior golfers in the world. He is really struggling now, shooting in the high 70s, low 80s, because he is going to college soon and he thinks he needs to develop a college swing versus a high school swing."

With my eyes rolling in my head, she continued.

"I think you are the right person to help him out. Would you be able to work with him?"

Of course I said yes and we made plans for him to visit me at David Leadbetter's academy. They came down to Florida within two days and I started working with him.

When I teach, regardless of playing ability, everyone goes through the same program. If I were teaching a clinic with the #1 player in the world, a college player, a high school player and a player that just wanted to break 90 more than two times a summer, they would all receive the exact same instruction. Literally, I could have 100 people lined up on a range with a bullhorn and have a successful clinic. Fluid motion is produced identically for everyone.

I therefore started Anthony in the same sequence

everyone goes through. I started off with a 30-minute whiteboard presentation of how fluid motion is produced, and then we hit the range. We dove into the first Fluid Cue, the nines. He hit five balls with it, turned to me and said, "I never want to leave this space."

I thought this was a good beginning and we continued going through the rest of the Fluid Cues. The two-day program went well, and he was sent off with a new understanding of his swing and of the game, and everyone felt satisfied.

Or so it seemed.

He had an excellent summer. He won one of the two biggest junior tournaments in the country and in September, he headed off to a great golf school. I didn't hear from him for six or seven months, or his mother whom I got friendly with, so I texted her at the end of the school year.

"Angela, how is Anthony doing? Did he have a good season at college?"

She immediately texted back and said he had a mediocre season. Angela was an excellent golfer and had played college golf. Being a successful player, she knew that my program, as long as someone had a solid swing, was the defining element in being successful in the game. She also knew her son's tendency to over-analyze his swing. Coupled with her husband's preoccupation with mechanics, she knew there was always a tendency for Anthony to get too technical.

Turned out she was right. Anthony had a mediocre golf season and was disappointed. Without saying it, both Angela and I knew exactly why this had happened.

He started to continuously work on his swing, and his coach, who was also very technical in his approach to the game, only encouraged that direction. I told her I think Anthony should come and visit me again, as he needed a refresher course. She had a tough time convincing her husband of this, as he was also was pre-occupied with mechanics and thought the only reason Anthony wasn't playing well was because something was wrong with his swing and that's a technical, not a mental, fix. I reiterated to her something she already knew, that I was not a mental coach, but a fluid motion coach.

She finally convinced him that it would be a good idea if Anthony did come and see me. I was in Iowa for the summer and they were about to travel to the east coast to play in some prestigious amateur tournaments, so visiting Iowa turned out to be not so far out of their way.

I met both of them at the course and we sat down and I started to give him the same presentation I had given him the previous year in Orlando. I could sense his father was very skeptical of what I was saying, as he lived in a technical universe with technical fixes. I smiled inside. After the talk, we went to the range and he started hitting balls.

I noticed his timing was off. As you know by now, timing is off when the cerebellum is compromised. The cerebellum is compromised when a part starts to overshadow the whole during a swing, so this was no surprise to me, as I immediately knew he had been working on his swing the moment he arrived on campus.

We went through the first set of cues again and within five minutes he had regained his timing. I was watching his father out of the corner of my eye and he started to have what I call, the jaw-dropping response, meaning he couldn't quite get a handle on what he was witnessing. Five minutes prior, Anthony's timing was off and then, almost miraculously, it was there. I could hear the wheels spinning in his head and I thought to myself, deal with it.

Between the time I saw Anthony for the first time and then saw him again, I had come up with the fourth set of Fluid Cues and I proceeded to teach it to him. He loved them. We then went on the course to practice and he played great. They left, both happy campers. Well at least Anthony, because what the father heard was a little threatening to his worldview of the game.

Anthony started to play very well and had some excellent finishes at some prestigious tournaments. At the end of the summer, he played in one of the biggest ones and was runner-up, which got him into a PGA tournament. It was a very successful run for him.

He returned to college. In May the following year, I texted Angela again and asked her how Anthony's season was. She said mediocre. "What do you mean?" I asked. "He was playing so great at the end of the summer—what happened?"

She said. "Well, he got back to school and immediately started working on his swing again."

I was speechless.

I said he should come and see me. She tried to convince him, but all he wanted to know was if I had a technique to help him work on his swing.

That is not only swing prison—this is solitary confinement within swing prison.

Anthony went on to have another mediocre season in his senior year, after three years ago being on the top of the amateur golfing kingdom. He is an extraordinary gifted golfer and one of the nicest kids you could ever meet. I only wish him the best of luck and perhaps one day he will be a superstar out there, but I don't have to tell you the moral of the story. It's obvious. How many talented golfers never reached their potential because they sentenced themselves to swing prison? Far too many.

Simplicity

9

Hitting the Wall

Everyone who has gone through the Fluid Motion Factor program, either in person or online, knows that somehow, one way or the other, the Fluid Motion Factor has to be accessed. This makes sense, as it is a universal process that produces a fluid, smooth and powerful swing for everyone. And they all learn a simple, repeatable way to access it. The program has gone through many iterations over the years, especially when I started teaching with David Leadbetter at his academy in Orlando. When you work with better players, it always elevates your own teaching, and as the old adage says, often the teacher learns more than the student.

This was certainly my case. But after working with some very good players, I was confused. As I mentioned, everyone that went through the program was convinced they have to access FMF, and everyone was satisfied they learned a simple way to do that.

But the program hit a wall. Some very talented

players could do the program on the range, in a practice round, but in a tournament situation, they were struggling. I was confused with this. If they were sold out to the program, which they were, and they knew how to do the program correctly, which they did, why couldn't they do it successfully in a tournament? After all, the program doesn't teach you to do something; it teaches you do less and less, until it feels like you are doing nothing. Why couldn't someone do that on demand?

After some reflection, I came up with the answer in one word.

Fear.

As someone who has competed his whole life in tennis, and is still competing, I knew this is what shuts you down when you play. Fear. I knew players who could do it on the range, and in practice rounds, but couldn't do it in competitive rounds, were experiencing fear. Most athletes have fear to a certain extent, but when it crosses a threshold, it will prevent the cerebellum from doing its job.

Fear doesn't show up because you are having a bad hair day. There is always a deeper reason why you are experiencing it. And the origin is not on the surface level, but rather buried deep within the mind. After some reflection, I came up with five origins of fear:

1. *Fear of failure*
2. *Fear of success*
3. *Playing for someone else*
4. *Not worthy*
5. *Not comfortable in one's own skin*

But this theory of mine, even though I knew it wasn't a theory, had to be field-tested to see if I was correct.

Here are some stories from the field.

I worked with a D1 team in Florida. They liked the program, especially the best player on the team. Fast-forward a year later and I am at a LPGA tournament watching one of my players, Gaby Lopez. I then see that top player from a distance and I go up to her and ask her how she is doing. "Selena" was excited to see me and said, "Fine." I said great! I asked her if she was still using the program and she said of course, but I am not getting the success I want. I said, "Oh really, do you want to talk about it?" Her response: "Yes!"

We found a quiet area and sat down. I could see she had a lot on her mind and asked her to tell me what was going on. She said she really enjoyed the program but had some challenges. I asked her what kind of challenges. She said she could access FMF on the range and in practice rounds but was having difficulty accessing it as consistently as she would like in tournaments.

Got it.

Just to make her comfortable, because I knew what was coming down the line, I repeated what she told me. "So, you can access it on the range, in practice rounds, but not as well as you would like in tournaments." She said yes, that is exactly the situation. I then asked her if she wanted to understand the problem from a deeper level, because I knew we were about to expose an open wound.

She quickly said, "Yes, I want to understand what is going on."

So, I asked her the million-dollar question: "Where does the fear come from?"

She froze for a split second, but quickly recovered. I could tell she was going into a deep, self-reflective mode.

What I asked her was perhaps the most penetrating and personal question you can ask an athlete, as it lays open one's soul. It is not like I knew her all my life; I didn't. Or that we had deep discussions about things in the past; we hadn't. But I felt she trusted me, so I took a chance and asked her.

She said, "I don't know."

I said, "Why don't you think about it and when you are ready, give me a call and we can discuss it." I then gave her a warm hug and said goodbye.

The next day I got a call from her. I was surprised. She said, "I have been thinking about our discussion and I want to tell you a story and see what you think. When I was growing up in my country, I was the best 10-year-old player. Nobody could beat me. I even beat players that are now on the LPGA Tour. But for some reason, I started playing poorly and the players I used to beat, started beating me.

"One day a group of mothers of the kids I was playing with came up to me and said, "You are not playing the way you used to play. Maybe you would be happier in another sport?"

I told her to stop right there.

"So, you are playing now, to show these mothers,

whom you probably don't even remember, that you are good enough to compete and win."

She said, "Exactly."

In the next three tournaments, she had a top five, a top 10 and a top 20.

The memory of that stinging statement that went deeply into the mind, heart and soul of a 10-year-old, so many years ago, was still pulsating. Even after all these years, she was playing for someone else, and not herself.

If someone can't access FMF, whether they believe in FMF or even know about FMF, it is because of a block. If the mind can only settle down to a certain level and then it hits a block, you will not be able to create the silent, abstract, holistic environment necessary for the subtle processes in the mind to sync the swing.

Because of that, you may never reach your potential, unless that block is removed. It doesn't matter how much you practice, how many lessons you take, or what you work on in your game, that block has to be removed. For her, it just took one conversation. For most it is not that easy, as you will now hear.

I worked with a professional player who has long since retired and moved onto another role in the industry. He heard about my program through David Leadbetter. This player was very talented, world class in every aspect. But after meteoric success, he stopped winning. Everyone was surprised, most especially himself.

One day we were playing on his home course. The course was empty. No one behind and no one in front, so we could take our time on every hole. We got to a short par four, and he teed it up, telling me he wanted to hit a high draw.

First ball, no high draw. Second ball, no high draw. Third ball, no high draw.

I was puzzled. I asked him, "What is going on?"

He paused for a second, as if he were debating whether to say what was on his mind. I felt he was either going to tell me something revealing or just not answer.

He answered: "After a while in my career, someone I deeply admired, a real legend in the game, started saying that I was the best ball striker he had seen since Hogan." And then he went silent, as he wanted both of us to reflect on what that meant.

I said, "So now every time you tee it up, you are trying to prove his statement correct."

Almost under his breath, he said, "Yes." It was almost a surreal admission of the frustration he had felt for so many years and finally was able to admit it to someone.

There were other reasons his career faltered. He tried to change his swing too many times, but certainly the almost unconscious desire to prove to someone he deeply admired, that what they said about him was correct, played a significant role. He was not playing for himself. He was playing for someone else. As a result, there was a block to accessing FMF. His mind could only settle down to a certain level, so his swing could only be synced to a certain level.

All of us have many levels; we are all complicated to a certain degree. But if you are an accountant or a teacher, you can hide those complications and still have a successful career. You may not be ideal all the time in your work, but you can still have a career. For a professional athlete, especially a professional golfer, you can't hide. Those complications will be revealed in your performance that day, and the next day when your results are published in the newspaper, and they may cost you your career. There is no place to hide, especially on the back nine on Sunday.

I think, and of course it is only my opinion, that 90 percent of the players on any of the major tours in the world, do not break through, not because of lack of skills, but because of the blocks in accessing deeper levels of silence under the gun. This has nothing to do with golf. This has to do with life.

What do you do? You know if this applies to you. Well, it's your challenge in life, because if you were blessed with high levels of talent in the game and fail to reach your potential, it's a frustrating feeling that may follow you for a long time. Here are my suggestions.

Change your diet. Eat organic food as much as possible. Eat as little meat as possible. Eat less fish and chicken, if you can. Less sugar. Eat more fruits, vegetables, and nuts. Drink more water. Avoid fast food and leftovers. Don't eat too late at night and sit for five minutes after eating, so the food can be properly digested. Diet is crucial in making the mind stronger and allowing you to cut through those blocks and access deeper levels of silence when you play.

Consider learning Transcendental Meditation. I

have been meditating regularly for 45 years. I meditate twenty minutes twice a day, morning and evening. It is the single most important decision I have made in my life because it affected all area of my life. And it can help your golf game. It will allow you to effortlessly culture more silence in your mind, on and off the course. Visit TM.org to learn more.

Start believing in yourself more. Don't doubt your abilities. Doubt kills. Forget what other people say about you or your game. Create your own environment. Consider closing the book on your swing. How many refinements do you want to make? Will it ever end? You know how to swing. Work more on accessing what you already own. Ask yourself this question: If I could access what I already own, would I be satisfied at the end of the day? Virtually all the players I have asked this question to said yes. If that is the case for you, work more on your short game. When Lydia Ko was number one in the world, 80 percent of the time she had a wedge in her hand when practicing.

Life on every level has challenges. We are here to grow, to learn, to gain wisdom and confidence. For most, this growth takes place in a personal space. For professional athletes, it takes place in a public space. You are exposed as a professional athlete. The world at large sees how you are doing in the classroom of life. You can't hide. In an office, there is always a place to hide. That is why successful athletes are to be admired, because in front of an audience, they are showing you how free they can be, when for most, that freedom would not be there. Perhaps this is why we admire the superstar athlete so much. Both the athlete and the audience, without acknowledging it, know that the ever-present fear that we all have as human beings has been transcended and someone has broken free from it and performed in a spectacular manner that elevates us all. Instantly, they become our role model, regardless of our profession, and inspire us to also be free from fear in our lives. And that is why they are probably worth every penny of all the millions or tens of millions they earn.

Summary

I mentioned in the beginning of the book, there are three paradigm shifts that form the basis of the program. Here they are:

1. *You are not trying to swing well, you are just trying to access what you already own.*
2. *A good swing does not break down. What breaks down is the ability to access the swing.*
3. *The more abstract criteria used in evaluating a swing, the better chance you have of accessing the Fluid Motion Factor. Conversely, the more concrete criteria used, the less chance you have of access-ing the Fluid Motion Factor.*

If you haven't made these paradigm shifts after going through the program, you will probably be in and out of using the program correctly. Interestingly enough, the highest use of the program is when you don't even need to use the Fluid Cues, because on that day, you were where you already needed to be on every shot. But that experience may be hard to find unless you know the money is in the bank and always available. It reminds me of the *Wizard of Oz*, when the wizard told those four marvelous characters that they already had what they were so desperately searching for.

Don't make the Fluid Cues the stars of the show. The stars of the show are that muscle memory does not break down and the brain physiology needs to operate in wholeness. Those are the most powerful Fluid Cues. Just thinking about these two concepts can change your game.

And my suggestion is to ask yourself how many years do you want to work on that swing of yours? Is the answer really in the dirt? When will it be done? Do you really want to be on an eternal quest? If you ask yourself whether you could access what you already own on a consistent basis, would you be satisfied? If you answer yes, then my suggestion is to spend the rest of your golfing career doing exactly that. It may be the best golf decision you ever made.

When you start going through the program, you are beginning on a journey toward simplicity. It is a journey of self-discovery. You will start being your own teacher. You will learn more and more about yourself and your capabilities out there. You will be exploring different dimensions about yourself and your game. You will go in and out of using the program correctly. This is inevitable for everyone as it doesn't matter how many times you tell somebody they can't own the program or it is a pattern-less pattern, the mind is wired such that it wants to go against these concepts.

So be patient with yourself. Be easy with yourself. If you do that, you will be consistent and of course enjoy the game more. Even better than low scores is enjoyment of the game. The ability to have freedom and not be a prisoner of the very strict boundaries that golf offers, is a beautiful, beautiful feeling and stays with you far longer than the score you put on the scorecard. It could affect other areas of your life, as there are boundaries everywhere in our lives. Transcending those boundaries is very much what life is all about.

It was a great joy writing this book, as it is the culmination of 45 years of studying a subject I love. In many ways it is autobiographical, as it describes my journey in sports and in life. Since sports has been and is still a significant part of my life, I hold on to the concepts and principles described in this book as things very dear to me. It was my pleasure in sharing them with you.

I'll end with one of my favorite stories. It clearly illustrates the power of our minds.

Jimmy Walker was a talented golfer but wasn't having much success. He and others knew he had the talent to make it, but the results weren't there. He got ahold of Butch Harmon's number and texted him, asking if he would be willing to work with him. No response.

A couple of months later, he texted again...no response.

Finally, Jimmy's wife took the phone and texted

Butch, saying we have texted you twice with no response, so please tell us one way or the other whether you will work with Jimmy, so we can plan our lives accordingly.

Five minutes later, Butch texted back, apologized for not responding earlier, and said he knew about Jimmy's talent and would be delighted to work with him.

The rest is history. Jimmy won three times in his first eight PGA tournaments in 2014, right after working with Butch. In 2019, one of the golf magazines interviewed him about his success and having Butch as his coach. They of course asked him about the swing changes Butch made.

Jimmy said we didn't do anything with my swing. He told me I had the talent to win on tour and that was all I needed to hear.

What a brillaint and poignant story. We are all probably much better than we think we are.

Opportunity for Personal Instruction

With this book, you are going to take a journey of self-discovery. Everyone goes through three learning curves in the program: range, course, and competitive golf. Because of that, and because the program is subtle and sometimes needs guidance, I am offering you an opportunity to have interactive video sessions with me.

There will be a few options. The first option will be four interactive individual or group video sessions, each lasting about an hour, depending on how many questions are asked. There will also be a subscription series available. The online video sessions will be recorded and archived, so they will be available for repeated viewing. During the video sessions, you will also learn refinements beyond what I could offer you in the book. I am also available for private and group clinics. In addition, there is an online video certification program available if you are interested in teaching FMF to your students.

Please email me for more information.

steven@stevenyellin.com

I want to hear from you about your progress with the program! When I teach someone and I watch them play, I get a vicarious thrill, because I know what they are experiencing inside. I would enjoy hearing your stories, as well.

Thank you for going through my program. It was an honor, privilege, and pleasure to share everything I learned in this marvelous journey of mine. Good luck with everything.

- Steven

Author Biography

Steven Yellin grew up in Florida where he was the Florida High School state singles tennis champion and a member of the championship team. He went on to have an outstanding career playing #1 singles at the University of Pennsylvania and was a member of the All-Ivy team in 1972. As a senior at Penn, in a challenge match, he had an experience that changed his life. It was a deep experience of the Zone. Over the next 45 years, he developed the Fluid Motion Factor program, which has been taught in twelve sports, including seven professional sports.

Steven has presented his program at some of the leading golf summits in the country, including the Golf Magazine Top100 Summit and the 2016 NCAA national college coaches' convention, as well as numerous PGA and LPGA sectional meetings. Steven has worked with players on the PGA and LPGA Tour that have won over $80 million in prize money and six major championships. His certification program has been taken by some of the top instructors in the world.